The Lecturer's Survival Guide

Serving as a comprehensive introduction to those new to teaching in higher education, this essential guide discusses pedagogical approaches that are current in higher education and the wider responsibilities of teaching within higher education. This book outlines the key aspects of navigating the role, including becoming a personal tutor and supporting the needs of a diverse student body. Readers will benefit from advice on promoting wellness, best practice while teaching and enjoying their role as they embark on their first academic job. It also underlines throughout that all lecturers need to be guided by a set of values around respect for students and the need to create learning environments that move away from any 'ghetto' style approaches to higher education. It suggests that our values as lecturers are key to us creating and exemplifying the much-needed ethical and just practice in our classrooms so that they mirror the kind of society we would like to live in and enable every student to feel as though they 'belong' at university.

Written in an informative yet accessible manner, chapters explore the following:

- The challenges of transitioning from student to lecturer
- The key theories that underpin successful curriculum design
- Assessment and feedback as a source of empowerment within higher education teaching
- The need for academic personal tutoring
- Staying well when teaching within higher education

Written for those who are new to higher education or to teaching in this setting, *The Lecturer's Survival Guide* is an essential read for any higher education teacher who wishes to ensure successful teaching whilst maintaining a healthy work-life balance.

Ann Marie Mealey has held multiple academic leadership roles in HE, including Academic Group Leader for the Humanities; Senior Teaching Fellow/Reader and Programme Coordinator for the PGCertHE at Leeds Trinity University, UK; and Associate Dean for Learning and Teaching (Teaching Enhancement) at GBS. She is currently Director of Catholic Mission at Leeds Trinity University – a role which requires her to embed the values of the university into its strategic objectives.

The Lecturer's Survival Guide

An Introduction to Successful Teaching in Higher Education

Ann Marie Mealey

LONDON AND NEW YORK

Designed cover image: Getty images

First published 2024
by Routledge
4 Park Square, Milton Park, Abingdon, Oxon OX14 4RN

and by Routledge
605 Third Avenue, New York, NY 10158

Routledge is an imprint of the Taylor & Francis Group, an informa business

© 2024 Ann Marie Mealey

The right of Ann Marie Mealey to be identified as the author of this work has been asserted in accordance with sections 77 and 78 of the Copyright, Designs and Patents Act 1988.

All rights reserved. No part of this book may be reprinted or reproduced or utilised in any form or by any electronic, mechanical, or other means, now known or hereafter invented, including photocopying and recording, or in any information storage or retrieval system, without permission in writing from the publishers.

Trademark notice: Product or corporate names may be trademarks or registered trademarks, and are used only for identification and explanation without intent to infringe.

British Library Cataloguing-in-Publication Data
A catalogue record for this book is available from the British Library

ISBN: 978-0-367-76056-4 (hbk)
ISBN: 978-0-367-76758-7 (pbk)
ISBN: 978-1-003-16843-0 (ebk)

DOI: 10.4324/9781003168430

Typeset in Galliard
by Apex CoVantage, LLC

Contents

Introduction	1
1 Challenges of Entering Into Higher Education: From Student to Lecturer	3
2 Basic Concepts Underpinning Good Curriculum Design, Active Learning and Imagination	21
3 Assessment and Feedback: A Constant Source of Empowerment Rather Than Imprisonment	43
4 Who Are Our Students?: The Need for Racial, Religious, Spiritual and Academic Personal Tutoring	66
5 Staying Well in Higher Education	90
Conclusion	102
Epigraph	*104*
Index	*105*

Introduction

We know that teaching matters. This is incontrovertible. We also know that those individuals who are attracted to a career in teaching in higher education are often those who are doing a PhD or who are in jobs aspiring to finance and complete a PhD so that they can land their dream job.

Getting into the HE sector is difficult in today's landscape due to the ambitious strategy that each university is trying to implement and achieve. Much of this focuses on student outcomes, employability, teaching quality and research excellence. Trying to demonstrate achievement in all of these areas can be very difficult and involve a lifetime of dedication and learning to get to a place where one could legitimately say that one can show achievement against all areas.

Those first steps from being a research student, or corporate businessperson, or stay-at-home parent to being a lecturer can be daunting – not least because the subject/module we might be asked to teach is new to us, thereby pushing us out of our 'comfort zone'. What can further make us feel uneasy is the general HE landscape itself as at first it might seem that there are so many terms and acronyms being discussed in meetings. It is easy to feel that if we were to speak out and say we didn't understand, we might have sealed our fate forever in the HE sector as being 'found out' as an 'imposter' who just didn't get it!

But the reality is that new lecturers are vital for the continuation of the contributions and academic achievements that others have brought to the university and to the sector more widely. The future is in the new appointments, those at the start of the journey towards having a permanent position at the university. So it makes sense that the more seasoned academic makes the time and effort to understand the new academic both as a person, as a professional, and as someone who needs to, at times, 'stand on the shoulders of the giants' who have had many years to grow and develop into the people that they are today. But growing people takes time. This is why we need to take time to support and to reflect on the ways in which we can help others to grow and develop in the current HE climate.

This is the main impetus for writing this book. After coming out of a 16-year post, which included teaching for that length of time, I felt that I needed to give

DOI: 10.4324/9781003168430-1

2 Introduction

something back to the teaching community. For a number of years, I was often very sad to bid farewell to esteemed senior professors who shared so much of their experience and knowledge about how students learn and how we can support them locally and more strategically in meetings. My sadness was not simply rooted in the fact that I would miss them as people but because there was no way to capture what they said or what they knew and pass it on to the new staff. Once such a person left, their wisdom and expertise left with them – unless of course they offered to mentor others or voluntarily stay in touch.

Furthermore, my experiences as a senior teaching fellow at Leeds Trinity and as an associate dean at Global Banking School for Learning and Teaching (Teaching Enhancement) brought me into contact with a large number of early career academics. Some had come from industry, some from PhD programmes, some from having taken a gap in their professional lives to focus on family and on children. But the key aspect that always stood out to me was the frequency with which I would hear the following phrases: 'I'm not a true academic but I think that . . . ' or 'I'm not sure if it's okay to say this but I think that . . . '

While some might say that this humility is a good characteristic to see, deep down it was often clear to me that there was a lot of uncertainty, elements of fear and self-questioning connected with taking up a teaching post at university level. Some people really did not feel worthy and were very aware of what they didn't know. Sometimes this feeling of what they didn't know was so strong that it overshadowed any feedback which I might have given on aspects of their practice which they clearly *did know* – and sometimes know very well.

PGCERTHE (Postgraduate Certificate in Higher Education) programmes are great for helping to ease people into their first academic role, but again, it depends on the atmosphere and who is in the group as to whether people feel they can genuinely ask anything they wish without the fear of being judged. Mentoring can also be a good way to induct colleagues into the running of a university, but if the mentor has not had the benefit of doing a PGCERTHE, or he/she is not familiar with the more strategic level initiatives that are going on in relation to learning and teaching, new staff can feel that their PGCERTHE is something separate to what they learn from their mentor. And sometimes what is said by a mentor might conflict with what is being said about current 'good practice' in teaching across the sector.

Having access to a book that might be seen as a guide which outlines some of the key pedagogical approaches that are current in the HE sector and which links these to the need for all academics to have a set of values around student learning might help the new academic in some small way. The approach taken to the writing of this book is to try to keep the new lecturer positive about their own purpose and expertise. It hopes to outline the expectations of the pedagogical community as regards teaching excellence and to suggest that our values are a compass for understanding the 'why?' of race equality, inclusive practice, staying well, supporting students and each other as we journey towards transforming the lives of our students one by one.

Chapter 1

Challenges of Entering Into Higher Education

From Student to Lecturer

After a 17-year career in teaching in higher education in the UK, I have decided to write this book. What I have come to learn over the years is that our lives as academic staff are so busy and the demands to do research, to achieve TEF Gold, to have fantastic NSS results, good module feedback and acceptable graduate outcomes are so intense that we very rarely get a chance to share what we know with our junior colleagues.

As we progress throughout a career, we sometimes get noticed by senior university leaders as being good at departmental administration, leadership and management, programme co-ordination, personal tutoring or committee work. Consequently, we can be asked to do more and more of this work. But the question we need to ask is, 'How much of what we learn doing all of these tasks is passed on?' Even if we are a mentor to a junior colleague, we may find that even these meetings are not enough for us to really make an impact on that person's career in teaching in higher education. Having a big impact on someone's teaching practice would involve a time commitment that is often not given to mentors – in spite of the fact that few would disagree about the overall significance of having a mentor.

In higher education, the demands are so great that we often find ourselves feeling that to be a good academic, we have to be all things to all people – including government and the newly established Office for Students. We sometimes fail to stop and reflect on what we do to ask ourselves, 'What would I say to my younger self?' 'What would I have liked to have been told when I was starting my career as a lecturer in higher education but nobody told me?' 'If I had one piece of advice or learning to share with anybody starting off their journey as an academic, what would it be?'

If you are reading this book as a veteran of learning and teaching, please ask yourself: 'What would I really like to pass on to my junior colleagues at my institution regarding a career in HE in general and, more specifically, regarding teaching and learning?' Or indeed another question you might ask is, 'Have I tried to pass on what I know to another colleague in order to enable them to know more than me, to be better, to achieve more or to serve our students more fully?'

DOI: 10.4324/9781003168430-2

4 Challenges of Entering Into Higher Education

This is a question which, in my opinion, few colleagues who are leaving the HE sector or retiring from it actually ask themselves. Indeed, the institutions that they are leaving very rarely ask that question either. Often, colleagues leave universities without being celebrated for the contribution that they have made to the institution, and if they are, colleagues are often recognised for their research more than for the number of lives they have transformed through excellent teaching and pastoral support by way of personal tutoring. Although all university vice-chancellors would agree that teaching and personal tutoring are absolutely essential to what higher education learning is all about, it would be interesting to know how many actually take the time to speak to experienced colleagues before they leave an institution to see what they have learned about how we can do these things better. Wisdom accumulated over years and years of interacting with students inside and outside of the classroom shapes our thinking, educates us about what works and what does not work in teaching as well as instructing us regarding what students really need as people too. This is one of the key reasons why it needs to be passed on.

Looking at Things From the Perspective of the New Lecturer

From the perspective of a new lecturer starting university, having access to the wisdom and advice of an experienced lecturer is invaluable. The role of the academic mentor is often considered to be key at the start of a new career in a new organisation. The mentor can also provide much needed support around understanding students, teaching, the priorities of the organisation and where to access relevant information such as a library and student support services. The mentor can also provide encouragement, motivation and understanding when the lecturer is experiencing difficulty or challenges around student learning, student satisfaction or institutional directives around teaching and learning that are new or novel.

Some institutions take pride in providing a mentoring programme for new staff, but oftentimes this is not extended to Ph.D students teaching one module, those covering sabbatical leave, part-time/sessional staff, or visiting lecturers. These staff often rely on the kindness of those on the faculty to help them out if they have questions regarding students or teaching. If, however, the module is scheduled and delivered as an evening class, oftentimes members of the faculty will not be in their offices, and this leaves the new member of staff very much to their own devices regarding what policies exist around student support, marking, teaching and learning practices or even expectations in the sector around what constitutes good teaching.

In such cases, the new member of staff may have to rely on reflecting on the experience of teaching that they had themselves at university and/or to emulate the teaching style of the best lecturer they had. Furthermore, because they are not full-time faculty members, 'some' occasional lecturers do not have the benefit of undertaking a Postgraduate Certificate in Teaching and Learning in Higher Education (PGCERTHE). And this adds to the lack of support available for new colleagues regarding learning and teaching.

A further challenge facing new starters has to do with the curriculum itself. Often, we begin our careers by inheriting a module descriptor that has been written by someone else, is not linked to our own research area, and which includes learning outcomes that perhaps are not so well aligned against the assessments for the module.

It can be a real challenge to one's confidence in teaching when one is teaching something that is outside our comfort zone (no matter how experienced we are). It can also be difficult to remain confident about teaching topics we are less familiar with when we are teaching it to bright and engaged university students who are expecting expert knowledge from the tutor. Of course, most lecturers are skilled in how to research topics from scratch, but it is a different matter when we are a page ahead and expected to deliver expertly to a set of highly intelligent undergraduates. Researching a topic is very different from teaching it. Consequently, confidence is a big factor in delivering an engaging and highly interactive session to university students. And if we lack confidence when we are teaching, there is always the worry that what could have been avoided had we had more support will end up in us being asked why our module satisfaction scores are so low. We may also be asked by senior university leaders why the open comments in the NSS, for instance, are suggesting that lecturers were not friendly and approachable or that they were not available when needed. The latter might well be the case because the tutor was not paid to answer emails during the week when they are only being paid by the hour by the university to cover some teaching for someone else. This can create a vicious cycle of worry for both new staff and for students.

Additionally, it shows that the challenges of being new to HE are many and indeed multifaceted and complex. However, ultimately, the starting point for new academics must be making that transition from being a student themselves and/or a researcher or professional in some career to being a lecturer in higher education. To do this, we need a resource or a support guide that will offer us the basic tools that we need to have in our toolkit as we start our career in higher education teaching and learning. This book is an attempt to do just this. It does not purport to answer everything, but it is an attempt to equip the new lecturer with some key pieces of HE pedagogy and wisdom that I have collected about the sector throughout my own career in higher education. It is my attempt to 'pass on' to the new generation of academics some of what I have learned so far in the hope that they will learn something from it and go beyond it in order to be better educators and to develop further than I did. We need to pass on what we know to others in the hope that they do what we did better – having the benefit of what we learned whilst being ready to understand and interpret what the new circumstances and challenges of higher education might be. So where to begin?

How Students Learn and What It's For

From my experience of delivering staff development sessions for new academics, it has become clear to me that there are several views prevalent in the academic community about how we define and explain the purpose of learning. For some, it is about getting a job and enhancing employability prospects. For others, it includes this aspect, but it also involves a focus on developing people, enhancing character, expanding the mind and/or giving students the tools to make a difference in the world.

The Catholic saint John Henry Newman (1801–1890) is known for his scholarly work on the purpose of the university. He points out that education is for a number of things, including cultivation of the mind, developing ideas and understanding how phenomena are interconnected and changing the world. He showed a critical view of university programmes that encouraged students to focus narrowly on one subject instead of looking forwards to a range of opportunities that might be available through the study of multiple subjects. This is because, in his view, education should be broad in scope and not simply based on outcomes or measurable assessment tasks.

He expressed the following in his first book (discourse 5) titled 'Knowledge Its Own End':

> It is a great point . . . to enlarge the range of studies which a University professes, even for the sake of the students; and, though they cannot pursue every subject which is open to them, they will be the gainers by living among those and under those who represent the whole circle. This I conceive to be the advantage of a seat of universal learning. . . . An assemblage of learned . . . [brought together] for the sake of intellectual peace, to adjust together the claims and relations of their respective subjects of investigation. They learn to respect, to consult, [and] to aid each other.
>
> (Newman 1990, 76)

To this end, Newman and those of his generation saw education as a noble endeavour and as aimed towards providing students with an opportunity to develop intellectually within an energetic and liberating philosophical culture in which all views are heard, debate is encouraged, and imagination is cultivated in the fullest possible sense (See Lanford 2019 for a summary).

The ancient Greek philosopher Aristotle saw education as being part and parcel of cultivating the virtues and promoting the common good (as perceived by the state or 'polis'). He was committed to the idea that with good education in the virtues and human behaviour, political life in the state would be better for everyone. Virtuous citizens would lead to a better state overall (Vo Van Dung et al. 2016).

The French philosopher and mathematician Descartes saw education as connected with the search for truth. Questioning truth and what might be perceived as the norm was a key part of the Cartesian philosophy. In *Principles of Philosophy*, Descartes claims that '[i]f you would be a real seeker after truth, it is necessary that at least once in your life you doubt, as far as possible, all things' (Descartes 1644).

Furthermore, he uses the metaphor of a tree to discuss what is noble in relation to the quest for knowledge. For him,

> the whole of philosophy is like a tree whose roots are metaphysics, whose trunk is physics and whose branches, emerging from the trunk, are all the other sciences, which may be reduced to the three principal ones, namely, medicine, mechanics, and morality.
>
> (Ariew 1992, 101)

Today, however, with our skills agenda and the government putting pressure on universities to demonstrate their significance in relation to preparing graduates for the job market, and with the introduction of student fees, the scene is less romantic. Frequently, we find academics responding to the question about why education matters by making statements such as 'because we need to ensure we close the skills gap', or 'because of social mobility', or 'because we need to ensure that everyone gets a chance to learn new skills and improve their career prospects and standards of living'

Clearly the responses are varied and multiple. It seems to me that as time goes by we hear less about the lofty ideas of Newman's thought being floated in the corridors of our universities and much more about the employability agenda and the need to ensure that we close the skills gap in society between different student demographics.

This is not to say that one would be deemed odd if one were to promulgate the view that education should enhance the mind and foster a vivid and enquiring imagination, but it is simply to say that the function and purpose of education seems to be less idyllic than it used to be and much more outcome focussed.

This is an important point to keep in mind when starting out on a new career in higher education as it helps the new academic to understand why targets in relation to student survey data and employability data are so significant. The graduate outcomes survey is clearly important for demonstrating the significance of degree programmes as it is thought to show that those who go to university will earn more in a graduate job than someone who did not go to university.

Additionally, the NSS data (National Student Survey) is frequently referred to by senior leaders in universities, especially if it shows high levels of student satisfaction with a programme of study as this is thought to prove that the teaching is good, the assessment is clear and fair and the student experience is positive all round on all programmes of study.

All of this, either directly or indirectly, will impact on what any university wishes to emphasise about its key institutional driver for any given year. One may think that this has little or nothing to do with teaching and how

8 Challenges of Entering Into Higher Education

students learn. But a poor rating by a cohort in the NSS survey, for example, can have detrimental effects on the recruitment for that programme in subsequent years, or it could lead to questions being asked about the standards of teaching, learning, and feedback for students on a given programme. Understanding the wider pressures around university metrics and data in advance of teaching a group of students can also help the new academic to survive in the community of practitioners and to be forearmed before going into a group of students to teach for the first time. But this is not to say that the data will tell us everything that we need to know about each student group.

Data and what constitutes 'good' practice in learning and teaching are always changing. And we need to get comfortable with this in HE. This explains, in part, why there is a need to understand the difference between 'knowing' and 'learning'. In short, we can refer to the former as being more unquantifiable and in a state of flux (perhaps even ever-changing) while the latter is something that can be tested and examined.

Dweck (2013) explains the distinction nicely in an article entitled 'Do you trust your ability to grow?' When we claim we *know* something, it is an 'inner knowing' that we sense. We may know or feel that we have grasped something, but it might not be measurable or quantifiable. This 'knowing' can also change over time because what we know today may be reinterpreted in light of new information or facts, and we have to revise this. Things are always in a state of flux or development. Nothing is static to the extent that it is fixed or unchangeable. As Dweck (2013) puts it, '[t]he things you know today are not enough. Facts change, new challenges arise, and so you can never think, "I know this" and call it done'. Problems and perspectives resurface and reform in different ways so we can never authentically claim that we are at the end of the journey of 'knowing'. We must always try to keep in mind that most things are in a state of flux.

This is an important point to remember when taking on teaching for the first time as it can help us to understand that what we include in our learning materials this year may and should be subject to change in subsequent years. It also helps us to understand that what we may think we know may in fact be questioned by our students if one of them knows more about a particular topic than we do. And we should not be intimidated or put off by this fact. Rather, we should expect that 'knowing' changes and that someone might know more than us about something.

Furthermore, expecting changes and being comfortable with not knowing everything highlights that we should be open to always seeing facts and information as ever changing, ever evolving and involving a lifelong quest for understanding. And, furthermore, we should be humbled by the fact that one of our students knows something more than we do about a particular topic. This is an occasion for co-creation and learning from students rather than one of embarrassment for the lecturer. Nobody knows everything. And we can

Challenges of Entering Into Higher Education 9

feel this acutely when we are teaching a module for the first time on a topic that is new to us too. But there is help all around us – including from the students at times. In addition to researching new topics that we are teaching, we should be open to learning from students too – especially in a task where we might have asked students to research a topic for themselves, as in student-led enquiry approaches to teaching.

All of this shows, therefore, that the distinction between 'knowing' and 'learning' is crucial to higher education pedagogy because it shows us that we should really refer more to 'learning' (and less to knowing) as 'learning' encapsulates more fully the idea that students (and tutors) are on a journey. It is not a single destination or outcome. Rather, there can be multiple outcomes along the way and a final assessment, but the learning should be seen in a creative and developmental way. To say 'I know' is to fail to acknowledge the continuous quest for understanding, requestioning, learning again and journeying towards truth and understanding.

But this developmental perspective is not without its challenges too. Because it is difficult to pin down what someone might have learned from our lecture, seminar, group tasks or module, it is often difficult to know how to assess this learning even though we know we must do so.

A key question, therefore, that we must always keep in mind regarding student learning is: 'How do I know that my students have learned?' 'What metrics will indicate that learning has taken place?' 'Will the students agree with my judgement of what they have learned and how well they understand it?' 'Will a second marker, moderator or external examiner agree with me?' 'What tasks should I ask my students to do in class so that I can test learning?'

These questions are of course ongoing, which again emphasizes the point that our reflection on how a module or unit of study is going for our students should involve active engagement and continuous reflection on whether we are setting students the right kind of tasks to assess their learning. Of course, we may not have the power (especially at the start of a career) to say what assessment should be set for a module or to completely 'own' the module in terms of module and assessment design, but we can and should take control of how we teach, assess and support student learning in our teaching sessions.

We can do this in a multitude of ways, including the following:

1. Groupwork aligned against the learning outcomes
2. Post-it Note exercises that allow students to post answers to a leading question on the wall of the classroom
3. Vevox quizzes, Kahoot, Mentimeter questions that allow students to answer questions about their learning in a more anonymous way through using their mobile phones
4. Asking leading questions to students about their learning

10 Challenges of Entering Into Higher Education

5. Drawing on students' experiences in life (constructivism) or on what they already know about a topic to test where we should begin 'new learning' with them
6. Blog posts, class debates for and against a particular claim or motion
7. Question and answer session which includes the lecturer and the entire class to test 'general understanding'
8. Online quizzes on Moodle or using other digital apps or platforms such as MS Forms on MS Teams.

In short, therefore, before we begin teaching a module, we need to be very clear in our own minds about which methods are best at helping learners to understand the key concepts of a module or unit of learning and to demonstrate to us, through assessment and other in-class activities, that they have actually learned. As Phil Race puts it,

> [w]e can only measure what learners *know* as far as we can assess the evidence of what learners produce. In other words, we can only measure what learners *show* of what they know. And what they show depends so much on what we *require* them to show in our various assessment contexts.
>
> (Race 2014, 10)

It goes without saying, then, that we must give learners as much information as we possibly can to ensure that they know what is required of them in terms of their learning and in terms of the assessment requirements. We must ensure that we are being as clear as possible about expectations and about the learning that we are expecting will happen in each session. We must also make sure that our learners are clear on what is being assessed. This is referred to as assessment literacy.

Assessment literacy is extremely important for all students but especially to our students who come to university from a range of backgrounds and with a range of experiences and learning. Some will have more of an idea than others of what is expected, but generally speaking, most students find that there is a change in expectations between secondary school and higher education. And they worry that they will not pass the assessment or even understand what is required to pass. Learners need to know exactly what is expected of the assessment and how they can be strategic in focusing their learning and demonstrating clearly to the tutor that they have met the learning outcomes of the module through the assessment task. Students need

> to be able to identify and clarify what is required of them in each of the different assessment contexts they encounter, and knowing how best to interpret relevant wording in published assessment criteria, learning outcomes and evidence-of-achievement specifications in course documentation.
>
> (Race 2014, 14)

In this regard it is often useful to hold 'assessment unpacking' sessions with students prior to the submission deadline for a piece of work as it will help to determine whether or not all students really understand what the assessment requires. Although it may be published in the module handbook or specification documentation, we cannot simply assume that the student has spent time interpreting these documents or indeed that the language that we are using in the assessment task is clear to students. Demystifying what is required of a task is often central to student success in assessment so that students, at the very least, are empowered to begin that task truly knowing what it is that they are being asked to do – rather than trying to 'guess' and hoping for the best once the work is submitted. The assessment should not be a 'guessing game' for students.

Although it is true to say that we cannot do it for them or to them, we can certainly increase as much as possible the chances of students being able to do it for themselves. Clear explanations of what is being tested and why helps students to become confident and more strategic about the resources they include in assessments, how they search for information, why they might refer to a particular source, and what they might want to argue in a piece of written assessment.

We might also say here that there is a moral imperative for tutors to help students to become fully literate about assessment tasks. As Meyer and Land (2003) point out, at times learning has to be really digested before it is truly understood. This takes time for students. Sometimes this digesting of concepts and learning is referred to as 'troublesome knowledge'. And given that it often takes time (more time than the duration of the module itself even) for students to fully understand certain concepts, then we must never leave them guessing as to what learning must be demonstrated in the assessment task. We must take the 'guessing' out of 'assessing'

Learning Takes Time: Some Other Useful Considerations

A further point that is also important to keep in mind when we begin a career in teaching in higher education is that learning takes time. While this may seem like an obvious point to make, it is relevant to understand how long our students are taking to grasp key concepts and terms that form part of their programme of study. Many academics argue, for instance, that year-long modules are to be preferred over semester-long modules. This is based on the view that the former gives students more time to digest material and to 'get to grips' with the content over a prolonged period of time whereas the latter expects students to learn at a pace – which doesn't always work for everyone. As Race points out, we sometimes need to spend a considerable amount of time reassuring learners that they are on the right track with their learning, and we may need to come to key pieces of information again and again before

12 Challenges of Entering Into Higher Education

students are competently able to make links between concepts, modules and units of learning (Race 2014, 10).

Linking learning together is often something that students struggle with (especially when they are new to higher education), and in a modular structure in particular, students may find it difficult to see how the modules on a given programme of study hang together. They may also find it difficult to see how their learning progresses from foundation year or first year through to the final year. Students are often unaware that what is learned in year one is crucial as it provides them with the key foundations stones upon which to build further learning as they progress to their final year.

This is a key point to keep in mind and to stress to learners in the early days of their programme. Sometimes students believe that since their first year results may not count towards their degree classification (and where they do, for instance, it is only in a minimalist way), their engagement doesn't really matter that much. It is important to stress to students from the outset that all learning matters as (particularly in level 4) it lays the foundations for other more complex learning later on. In short, learning needs to be slow, oftentimes repetitious and built around key concepts that are returned to later on in order to introduce more complex learning. This is often referred to as a spiral curriculum – where tutors will go back to key concepts and expand and develop these further later in a degree programme or at different intervals.

These points are also key to recall when designing new modules or a programme, for example. Although it is unlikely that a new lecturer would be leading a periodic review or a programme revalidation or validation, it is worth noting from the outset how the curriculum one is teaching has been designed. It is important to ask, 'Is it a spiral curriculum?' 'Is it skills led?' 'Or is it content led?'

Asking these key questions can help the tutor to know in advance of teaching the students how much groundwork they need to put in at which level of study in order to meet the module and/or programme level outcomes. Understanding the rationale for module/programme design can really help lecturers to have a good overview of the entire student learning journey, and this makes them more competent about what they can and cannot expect learners to know at key points in the learning journey.

Of course, we cannot always assume that the person who led the design of the curriculum will still be working in the department – or available to answer questions – but a good programme leader should be able to work out what kind of design models have been used when the curriculum was being put together so that they can advise new staff about this. The best advice perhaps that can be given to the new academic here is to ask about the design of the programme and how the modules fit together from the programme leader or head of department. This will be particularly pertinent if the programme relies on programme level assessment rather than modular assessment. While we should always try to understand how a module fits into the overall programme structure, we should also understand how programme level assessment

Challenges of Entering Into Higher Education   13

encourages students to see individual bits of learning as part of a 'bigger picture' as regards what it means to hold a degree in a particular subject.

A further piece of advice that might be given to the new lecturer here is the fact that we should not go into every class absolutely determined to discuss every single slide that we have prepared for our students. We should always be open to 'testing the waters' to determine whether students are really engaged with and understanding what we are trying to teach them. If we need to spend more time than expected on a particular idea or concept, then we should try to do that – particularly if it is a key concept that forms part and parcel of what is believed of what a student on a particular programme should be able to do and/or understand. In this sense, we should always be engaging with the 'student voice' to determine whether learning is actually happening. We need to always find out from students what they have learned and go from there as regards to determining what our own next step needs to be.

Activities such as Post-it Note exercises where students write some key positives and areas for development of a module on a Post-it Note for the lecturer are important here. Digital learning apps such as Kahoot and Vevox are also useful as they allow lecturers to ask students whether learning is happening and what they need more help with without students actually having to say it themselves or reveal their name to the lecturer. These kinds of activities always help to create an 'open dialogue' between the lecturer and the student regarding how well the learning is going. As Neary and Stephenson's work demonstrates, these kinds of activities create a 'collaborative relationship' between the student and the lecturer which results in a bond of trust being built up where significant academic work can take place (Bell et al. 2009, 97ff).

The term 'students as partners' is linked to all of this collaboration and is one that all lecturers will hear a lot about. And this narrative is likely to continue. Creating a good rapport with students in the teaching space ensures that students will feel able to give feedback on all aspects of their learning to the lecturer rather than having to endure a full module before they can include their views in a module evaluation feedback form, for instance. When the latter happens, it is too late for the lecturer to address any areas of dissatisfaction. However, when we treat students as partners, we create an environment where they should feel able to let us know what their needs are as regards their learning. We must see students as our partners and treat them as such in the learning environment. Healey et al. describe this as 'a relationship in which all involved – students, academics, professional services staff, senior managers, students' unions, and so on – are actively engaged in and stand to gain from the process of learning and working together' (Healey et al. 2014, 12).

When we work together with students, everybody gains. Lecturers can get reassurance that learning is genuinely happening, and they can quickly address any issues facing students before they escalate to higher authorities at the university or end up in institutional data collected about the programme or module. Acting quickly on student feedback has benefits all round but primarily for the students as this open dialogue ensures that they feel able to voice concerns

14   Challenges of Entering Into Higher Education

and challenges to the lecturer in spite of any perceived power dynamics that might be at play in the minds of the students.

This concept of students as partners also chimes with the 2002 paper published by HEFCE (Higher Education Funding Council for England). In relation to widening participation the paper refers to 'stretching the academy' so that education can be offered to a much broader range of students from a much more diverse student demographic. In this regard, HEFCE states that 'education must be a force for opportunity and social justice, not the entrenchment of privilege' (HEFCE 2002).

This 'entrenchment of privilege' must be something that we should always bear in mind when we are teaching. Some of our students do not feel entirely at home at university, especially in the first semester. They may feel as though they don't belong in the academy, or be overly conscious of being the first in their family to attend university. They could also be a mature learner who has had bad experiences of learning prior to starting university. In this regard, we must do everything that we can to ensure that they feel comfortable asking whatever questions they need to ask in order to feel fully supported in their learning. If we take time to create that environment where students understand from the outset that they are allowed and encouraged to be a partner to the lecturer, and that this includes giving constructive feedback to the latter, students can feel more involved in their own learning journey. Helping students to feel like authentic 'partners' in their learning helps the lecturer to determine whether extra input is required to ensure student success and satisfaction.

This is particularly apparent when it comes to understanding assessment. Our students, especially in the first semester of their programme of study, can often be in need of additional help and support in order to genuinely interpret and understand what is required of an assessment task. It's important that we explain the task clearly to students. We also need to be mindful of the fact that we ourselves are already part of a community of practice in our own discipline and that (either consciously or subconsciously) use language and terms with ease and which imply an implicit familiarity with our disciplines. We need therefore to remember that while some of our students might be very aware of what is required (either from parents or friends who are graduates), others are not. They do not come from backgrounds where they are 'cue-conscious' of what might be required at university at all, not to mention the assessment task.

In this regard, some scholars, such as Polanyi (1998), speak about 'tacit knowledge'. Tacit knowledge is considered to be implicit in the process of understanding assessment, for instance. This means that there is a certain implicit language or 'cue-consciousness' that is implicit in subject disciplines and in the language of assessment tasks that takes time to understand and interpret. Academic staff are thought to have this 'tacit knowledge' because they have spent years being immersed in their subject and in assessments tasks connected with it. Students will (with the correct help and support) eventually come to know and understand what this 'tacit knowledge' is all about even though it is extremely difficult to express in words (Cf. Bloxham and Boyd 2007, 70–71).

To put it differently, defining, interpreting and understanding words such as 'critically analyse', 'carefully review', 'demonstrate', 'evaluate' is difficult for students. Such terms may remain a mystery to those students who do not grasp the 'tacit knowledge' that is required to be successful in their subject discipline. We must always strive therefore to ensure that we are not keeping students locked out of the 'rules of the game', so to speak, but that we are ensuring at all times that they are given every opportunity to understand what the requirements of assessment are. Moreover, we must ensure that any inequalities or advantages that other students may have in terms of being more 'clued up' on expectations are eradicated as soon as possible. This is to ensure that our classrooms are inclusive and free from practices that may perpetuate injustice of any kind. As Bell et al.'s (2009) work emphasizes, we need to constantly enquire whether we are supporting a prejudicial and discriminatory ethos or learning environment that excludes and/or does not fully understand [for example] mature learners, students from lower socio-economic backgrounds or communities (p. 99ff).

All of this demonstrates why values are so important in the student journey. Either consciously or subconsciously, our behaviours and/or teaching practice and support mechanisms in our teaching spaces can be the reason why students remain positive and engaged or whether at times they may feel as if they don't belong at university or that they cannot succeed. The ways in which we provide inclusive spaces for students to feel empowered to inform us that they do not understand something or that we are not explaining things in the best possible way really matters for the success of our students. In fact, it is of crucial importance – particularly to those to who are less confident or who are still questioning whether or not they really belong in the academy.

Although it may seem odd to those embarking on a career in teaching in higher education to be reading about the need for ethics in their work at all times, many would argue that having a good set of values that are genuinely committed to student success and the commitment to making a difference in the lives of others are key to being an excellent lecturer. Field's work, for example, demonstrates clearly the need to be ethical and inclusive in all that we do as lecturers. For Field, nontraditional students take a big risk entering the 'academic ghetto' and usually suffer from lower attainment and poorer degree outcomes than students from what might be classed as more conventional backgrounds (Field 2003, 26).

While Field's research was carried out some years ago now, it is still very relevant for the contemporary lecturer to remember, especially if he/she wishes to avoid their own experiences of higher education being their primary or only

16 Challenges of Entering Into Higher Education

reference point, which directs how they interact with their students. As lecturers we must always strive to understand 'otherness', 'difference', 'newness', and be open to 'revising' what we previously thought worked in our practice. Education should never be a 'ghetto' but should provide a place where 'ghettos' are challenged and eradicated and where difference and diversity can be explored, celebrated and taken as an opportunity for us all to learn and grow as ourselves and as part of a learning community. In an ideal world, the classrooms of the academy should mirror the society we would like to see – with everyone having equal access to education and their specific story being accepted and valued.

Motivation and Keeping Students Going: Reminders From Phil Race

Finally, it is worth sharing some insights on how to keep students going, especially in times of challenge. From experience, students often get quite anxious coming to the end of a semester when deadlines are looming and the reality of having to demonstrate what has been learned hits home. At certain points, students will need lots of encouragement – not so much about anything structured about their learning but just as human beings. It is human to feel anxious about a new challenge or slightly nervous when we are undertaking something for the first time. For some students, there is a lot at stake when it comes to doing well and achieving good results at university, so they need support to keep going in times when perhaps the challenge is particularly taxing or they are also going through something personal in their own lives. This is where the role of the personal tutor is crucial and where students really need to see the 'human face' of the university (Yale 2019, 533ff).

The reasons why students need support can vary, but we need to be offering it to them. For some students, 'support is indeed critical' (Race 2005, 25). When confidence levels are low too, having a tutor who is supportive and believes in the student's ability to overcome their challenges and worries and succeed is a great source of encouragement. In fact, it is not uncommon to hear stories at graduations and years later about students who claim that they could not have succeeded or persevered to the end of their programme without the support and encouragement of their tutor.

But this support comes in multiple forms. Sometimes it is through our written feedback that we give it; other times it is personally by way of encouragement and support. All of our interactions need to be carefully thought through and reflected upon as it can be far too easy to brush off student support as something which is the remit of professional services departments and not those on the academic delivery side of the student journey.

This is a reminder to us to be careful about the phrasing of feedback or even our own words verbally to students – even when we might be disappointed

Challenges of Entering Into Higher Education   17

about the standard of work that has been submitted or the type of questions that students are asking about the assessment, for instance. A positive attitude is needed at all times so that we do not crush any student's confidence and that we are always seeing our role as educators as including a moral duty to respect the student who is looking for our support and help. This brings us back to values once again and to the need to see our students as 'partners' in the fullest sense of the word.

A second factor to remember in relation to student motivation is that what motivates some students is the desire at all costs not to fail or to prove someone wrong (Race 2014, 25). This is possibly a negative type of driver vis-à-vis education and learning, but it can be a motivating factor for some students which we need to be aware of. When students have been told they will 'never be successful in life' or a previous teacher has told them that they won't make it to university, this can actually drive students to prove that person wrong. Some students are out to prove something! In such cases their internal motivation is very high indeed.

The final factor identified by Race as being significant in relation to student motivation has to do with 'need' (Race 2014, 25). Students are often driven to keep going at something until they understand it fully because they simply need to. They need to graduate. They need to pass. They need a particular skill. They are running a business already and they need more skills in order to develop the business further for example. In short, frequently students need to understand something in order to become credible in a profession. 'Learners who take ownership of a particular *need* to learn are quite robust – they are not easily stopped, even by critical feedback when they get things wrong' (Race 2014, 25).

More recently, Race has come back to the need for lecturers to be the 'catalysts' for learning and for learners to have more motivation. He states that

> whatever we do to help learning to take place, we should regard ourselves as catalysts to the process, making it faster (that kinetics), more complete (that's about the position of equilibrium), less arduous (possibly by reducing the activation energy needed to get learning underway.'
>
> (Race 2020), Catalysing learning? – Phil Race (phil-race.co.uk))

We also need to ensure that whatever we do, it is also fun and enjoyable for learners so that they continue to want to learn with us.

We need to find fun ways that will help us to explain to students *why* they need to understand the learning outcomes, group tasks or formative activities so that students can become more committed about their need and desire to learn. The clearer and more engaging we can be with students about what they are learning, the better. This will reassure all students but be especially comforting those who need to always see that they are getting closer and closer to

18 Challenges of Entering Into Higher Education

their personal goal with each lecture or piece of assessment. This is what Fazey et al. (1998) call 'goal-orientation' to keep students motivated. Students need to understand everything so that they themselves can come to see that there is a point to the learning and that it will lead them to their desired outcome.

Understanding *why* a module is important to a student's future career is a key driver for a lot of students as they are motivated to understand concepts much more when they see its relevance for the world of work and/or for their future success. Linking back to Newman's understanding of education to change the world and Aristotle's stress on learning as part of becoming a virtuous person, we can see that although these are noble outcomes, we also need to combine these outcomes with the employability agenda.

Making learning relevant is essential for student motivation as not all students are happy to take a risk on studying a subject just 'for its own sake' as they worry about what career trajectory they might be able to take after graduation. In any case, irrespective of what programme of study a student undertakes, the lecturer should make the links between the module learning outcomes and the overall programme aims, which should also include a focus on employability skills. If it is not clear to students how their module will contribute to the employability agenda, as academics we should be able to make it clear for them.

Linking a module to the employability agenda is perhaps more straightforward in a placement module and less so in a module that is more conceptual or philosophical in nature. However, even if a module is more conceptual in nature, we should be able to demonstrate to students how this can help in the world of work. Problem solving, dealing with abstract concepts, challenging our worldview with alternative perspectives or global or culturally challenging information are all essential skills in any work environment, and this should be pointed out to students in the modules that we teach.

This is an area which the Office for Students is really keen to promote. They dedicate considerable time and resource to working with universities so that university provision continues to focus on skills development that is informed by trends from government and sectors of society where there are skills gaps for example. Their work includes funding certain conversion courses into subjects which are new and in demand, such as artificial intelligence and data science. Short courses focussed on key skills that are currently in demand are also encouraged along with the degree apprenticeship, which is a very clear way of providing graduates with the route into a specific profession while they work and study at the same time (supply of higher level skills – Office for Students).

But the focus on employability and keeping skills up to date should also be something that we continue to reflect upon in our own professional development as academics. We should always be searching for new knowledge and reflecting back on the content and methods used in a particular module year after year to ensure that we are deepening our own understanding not only

Challenges of Entering Into Higher Education 19

of the discipline but of the ways in which we are teaching the material to our students. We need to always enquire about whether our material is inclusive, international, sufficiently challenging and up-to-date, relevant and employer focussed, so that we do not become complacent in our own learning and impart this kind of complacency to our students. Teaching should be seen as a vocation that requires us to have a sincere commitment to always learn and grow ourselves and to be attuned to the needs of our students so that they can do the same. This does not mean that we need to always be perfect, but at the very least if we are committed to the task of learning, we will still see our failures as opportunities to learn and grow.

In the modern context, scholars are trying to find more ways of understanding how digital platforms and technologies can assist with student motivation. Since Covid-19, the world has changed. And so has the student learning and the way in which it is understood. Digital is no longer an add-on or a 'nice to be able to do' approach. Rather, digitally enhanced learning is a must. As Greg Kessler's recent work reminds us, we must think about ways of engaging students (no matter what their motivation for being at university might be) in their learning. We need to understand their social practices online too in order to find ways of using social media, for instance, as a tool for learning. Working collaboratively with students as co-creators of knowledge in a digital space can be very engaging and rewarding as different students can take the lead on different topics if a digital platform is managed carefully. Kessler argues that

> we have new opportunities to provide participants with immediate and salient feedback that can guide them as they co-construct knowledge with other members of these social communities. Throughout this co-construction of knowledge, participants share ideas and negotiate the nature of the construction itself.
>
> (Kessler 2019, 42)

And in this co-creation of new knowledge and learning, the tutor learns too. In this sense students are not only our partners but they are also our peers 'in learning' – as we are 'all' students together but simply at different stages of our own personal academic journey. Consequently, we must all learn to keep our enthusiasm alive for ourselves as academics and for those whom we are currently teaching. Enthusiasm inspires others. Enthusiasm keeps hope alive. As Henry Ford (1863–1947) puts it,

> [y]ou can do anything if you have enthusiasm. Enthusiasm is the yeast that makes your hopes rise to the stars. Enthusiasm is the spark in your eye . . . and the energy to execute your ideas. . . . Enthusiasm is at the bottom of all progress.

20 Challenges of Entering Into Higher Education

Bibliography

Ariew, R. 1992. "Descartes and the Tree of Knowledge." *Synthese* 92/1: 101–116.

Bell, L., M. Neary & H. Stevenson (Eds.). 2009. *The Future of Higher Education: Policy, Pedagogy and the Student Experience*. London: Bloomsbury PLC. ProQuest Ebrary (accessed 15/11/2021).

Bloxham, S. & P. Boyd. 2007. *Developing Effective Assessment in Higher Education*. Berkshire: McGraw Hill Open University Press.

Descartes, R. 1644. *Principles of Philosophy*. The Principles of Philosophy by Rene Descartes – Full Text Free Book (Part 1/2). www.fullbooks.com (accessed 02/01/2021).

Dweck, C. 2013. "Do You Trust Your Ability to Grow?" Interview, 27/09/2013. http://nilofermenrchant.com/2013/09/27/do-you-trust-in-your-ability-to-grow/ (accessed 29/12/2021).

Fazey, Della & John Fazey. 1998. *Perspectives on Motivation: The Implications for Effective Learning in Higher Education*. London: Routledge.

Field, J. 2003. "Getting Real: Evidence on Access and Achievement." In M. Slowley & D. Watson (Eds.) *Higher Education and the Lifecourse*. Maidenhead: Open University Press, SRHE.

Healey, M., A. Flint & K. Harrington. 2014. *Engagement Through Partnership: Students as Partners in Larning and Teaching in Higher Education*. York: Higher Education Academy. www.heacademy.ac.uk/engagement-through-partnership-students-partners-learning-and-teaching-higher-education (accessed 29/10/2021).

HEFCE (Higher Education Funding Council for England). 2002. *Partnerships for Progression*. No. 49. Bristol: HEFCE.

Kessler, Greg. 2019. "Promoting Engagement Through Participatory Social Practices in Next Generation Social Media Contexts." In Adesope Ousola & A.G. Rud (Eds.) *Contemporary Technologies in Education: Maximizing Student Engagement, Motivation and Learning*. Cham, Switzerland: Palgrave Macmillan, 41–48.

Lanford, Michael. 2019. "The Idea of a University." *The Literary Encyclopaedia*. www.litencyc.com (accessed 29/12/2021).

Meyer, J.H.F. & R. Land. 2003. "Threshold Concepts and Troublesome Knowledge 1 – Linkages to Ways of Thinking and Practicing Within the Disciplines." In C. Rust (Ed.) *Improving Student Learning – Ten Years On*. Oxford: OCSLD.

Newman, John Henry. 1990. *The Idea of a University*. Notre Dame: University of Notre Dame Press.

Polanyi, M. 1998. *Personal Knowledge: Towards a Post-Critical Philosophy*. London: Routledge.

Race, P. 2005. *500 Tips for Open and Online Learning*. London & New York: Routledge.

Race, P. 2014. *Making Learning Happen: A Guide for Post Compulsory Education*. London: Sage.

Race, P. 2020. "Catalysing Learning' Catalysing learning?" *Phil Race*. www.phil-race.co.uk (accessed 11/03/2023).

Van Dung, Vo, Do Thi Trang & Bui Thi Khanh Vy. 2016. "Aristotle's Educational Ideas." *European Journal of Education Studies* 2/9: 115–126.

Yale, A. 2019. "The Personal Tutor-Student Relationship: Student Expectations and Experiences of Personal Tutoring in Higher Education." *Journal of Further and Higher Education* 43/4: 533–544.

Chapter 2

Basic Concepts Underpinning Good Curriculum Design, Active Learning and Imagination

Introduction

In the previous chapter, we discussed the importance of understanding some key nuggets of information concerning why some HE institutions prioritise a particular agenda and what can be learned from experience about how to begin a career in HE.

We can have so many assumptions about who students are, how we will teach them, and we sometimes rely on our personal experiences of learning that can often be the polar opposite of the experiences of our learners today. This reminds us of the need to be humble, to listen and to re-engage again and again with what students teach us for us to continue to adjust and adapt our practice and to support their learning.

This listening to students is vital. And while we may not always like or want to adjust practice based on their feedback to us, we must challenge ourselves to see the world through their lens or perspectives. It might be likened to looking at a beam of light from the sun that shines into the centre of a room. The light is seen differently depending on where you are standing in the room. It may also look different depending on whether you are looking at it through different windows. All perspectives on that beam of light in that room, though distinct, are significant when it comes to doing good teaching. Every perspective matters. And all types of feedback from multiple stakeholders – including students – really matters too. It helps us to grow and adapt in our practice so that it continues to serve its purpose in support of student learning.

This chapter will continue the theme of this book, which is to ensure that new lecturing staff are as informed as possible regarding what to expect in the HE environment. It will begin to drill down into some key approaches to learning that – without having studied education – some subject experts may not have previously been familiar with. These terms will undoubtedly come up in contexts or meetings where topics such as curriculum design, approaches to learning, progression and student learning are being discussed. It is important therefore that those who are new to HE understand the ground upon which they are standing when they begin their teaching career. The hope is that academics can feel more empowered about the language and some of the key

DOI: 10.4324/9781003168430-3

concepts that will continue to form part and parcel of their environment and discussions throughout their career. The first of these foundational approaches to learning is Bloom's taxonomy of learning.

Introducing Bloom's Taxonomy of Learning: Concepts and Criticisms

We know from experience that we cannot possibly expect our learners to be advanced critical thinkers from day one of their student journey. Students need time to develop the necessary skills in order to demonstrate in a measurable way what they have learned and show what they can do. Nancy E. Adams (2015) explains this by using the example of primary school. She uses the example of learning our multiplication tables to show how 'rote learning' differs from the actual application of this learning. Solving problems using the multiplication tables requires different skills than those required from actually learning the tables in the first place (p. 152). In reality, therefore, a teacher could assess and test knowledge and skills in either of these types of thinking by asking students to tangibly demonstrate those skills in action. Ways of doing this might include oral examinations, groupwork, case studies that require problem solving, online quizzes, class debates – in other words, by *doing* something that is measurable in some way (p. 152).

This explains why Bloom's taxonomy is so important and continues to inform HE practice in curriculum design in particular. The taxonomy categorises skills that might be considered quite basic to ones which may be considered much more advanced, for instance. Some scholars subsequently categorised Bloom's work into higher-order and lower-order skills, in order to draw out more fully the precise distinctions between what we might initially expect from learners who are new to a subject and our expectations as regards those who are at more advanced levels of study. But it is important to note that higher-order and lower-order distinctions are not derived directly from Bloom's work (Adams 2015, 152). According to Gershon, Bloom had a very holistic view of education and what it is for and how learning is measured, and he agreed with the broad categories of learning contained within the classifications designated by cognitive, affective and psychomotor processes of learning (Gershon 2018, 4).

Bloom's own categories are as follows: knowledge, comprehension, application, analysis, synthesis and evaluation. Each of these categories was considered to represent a level of thinking, understanding and learning. The ordering in the following section makes it more clear in relation to student progress along a scale of learning.

Level 6 – Evaluation
Level 5 – Synthesis
Level 4 – Analysis

Level 3 – Application
Level 2 – Comprehension
Level 1 – Knowledge

(Gershon 2018, 5–6)

When we think about students having knowledge, we equate this with verbs such as 'describe' or 'demonstrate.' What we are looking to measure in student learning at this stage is their ability to demonstrate some basic understanding of a subject and/or task that will enable the lecturer to be satisfied that a basic understanding of key concepts, for instance, is present.

Comprehension is the second category of Bloom's taxonomy. This category refers to students being able to move beyond merely memorising things to a more complex understanding of concepts. They come to understand the concept in a much more in-depth way. At this point it is expected that learners should be able to explain the concepts to others and/or write about them using their own words, application and imagination. It goes beyond merely knowing things by heart.

This in turn leads to the third category, which is called 'application'. In this category, students should be able to apply what they have learned to specific issues or problems. 'An example of *application* familiar to medical librarians [for instance] is the ability to use best practices in the literature searching process, such as using Medical Subject Headings (MeSH) terms for key concepts in a search' (Adams 2015, 152). It is at this particular stage that student learning might be referred to as 'applied knowledge' Students begin to 'execute', 'implement', 'interpret', 'operate', 'problem solve' 'schedule' and 'sketch' out topics. The latter verbs are often the ones that are used in learning outcomes.

After this application stage, we find Bloom's attention focussing on learning in relation to a learner's ability to 'analyse', 'draw new connections between ideas', 'organise', 'compare', 'contrast', 'distinguish', 'examine' and 'question'. Here we clearly see a progression in relation to the expectations of what learners should know and can also see how the other levels have in fact paved the way for them to be able to reach this kind of level.

Finally, and this is often the most difficult level for new learners to come to grips with, we find the verbs 'analyze' and 'create' making the link between learning outcomes and assessment tasks. This level of evaluation would not really be expected of a new learner, but it is something that we need to be focusing on engendering in our students' skills-set. It is key for the employability agenda. When we reflect on what a graduate in philosophy, business, tourism, science or leadership should have, we notice that critical ability is key to developing graduates who can create new knowledge, critique things, find creative solutions to market demands, and see the need for new ideas, change or progress in a business. These skills are therefore vital for any graduate to have if they are to be employable and if our role as lecturers is to be credible and carry out what we claim to be delivering in our programme and module

24 Good Curriculum Design, Active Learning and Imagination

level learning outcomes. But the skills of analysis assume that the skills around application and knowledge have been mastered. Whereas application is concerned with 'how a student can take their knowledge and understanding of something and apply it in novel (and sometimes familiar) situations' (Gershon 2018, 7), analysis involves us 'being able to apply that which we know and show new connections, new understandings, new ways of working' (p. 7).

A final point worth mentioning here in relation to the taxonomy is that even when learners are engaged in the higher-level skills of evaluation and critical thinking, the lower-level skills are still included at this point. Another way of putting this might be to say that it is impossible to critique and engage in higher levels of evaluation unless one has the foundation upon which to base that critique. An example from the healthcare profession is offered by Nancy E. Adams when she says: '[i]t is important to recognize that higher-level skills in the taxonomy incorporate many lower-level skills as well'. So for example, if one wanted to ask students to evaluate medical literature on a topic (evaluation), such a task would be based on the premise that students already had the *knowledge* and *comprehension* (i.e., lower-level skills) needed to be able to 'apply' (application) their learning to the texts and *analyse* them as a nurse would do and 'to isolate the various components of internal validity such as blinding and randomization' (Adams 2015, 152–153).

Gershon uses the example of analysing how an engine works to demonstrate exactly the same point as Adams does in relation to the nursing profession. He states the following:

> For example, we might ask a group of students to analyse how an engine works. To do this, they would need to examine the engine in detail, looking at how the parts connect together, looking at what causes what and how the different parts influence and interact with one another. Without a prior knowledge and understanding of engines and engine parts, a knowledge and understanding which students feel confident applying to different situations, this task will be very difficult. Students might be able to point to how things within the engine connect to affect each other . . . but without a degree of mastery over the underlying facts and principles, they will struggle to accurately analyse the structure of the engine to any meaningful degree.
>
> (Gershon 2018, 7–8)

Put simply, then, the journey of a particular student from the learning outcomes to the assessment task in which they are able to show that they have mastered the lower levels of comprehension is a *process*. Within this process, students will also hopefully show that they are now ready to engage critically with higher levels of creative thinking that could lead to new knowledge that involves *both* levels together. One builds on the other.

The significance and prominence of Bloom's work cannot be underestimated in the current HE environment. As Brett Bertucio (2017) asserts, '[i]t

Good Curriculum Design, Active Learning and Imagination   25

has become impossible for pre-service teachers and their instructors to imagine lesson planning without those ubiquitous "action verbs"'. This means that we need to think carefully about what we ask students to do in class, what we say to them about learning outcomes, and how we explain what is required of them as regards the assessment *of* learning and assessment *for* learning.

An assessment task that is aligned against an outcome with verbs such as 'demonstrate', 'show' or 'outline', for instance, requires students to do a very different thing than verbs that are asking students to 'create', 'evaluate' or 'appraise'. Therefore, we need to prepare students step by step to meet the higher-level requirements by, first of all, meeting the lower-levels ones and progressing forward from there.

There are clear advantages to using Bloom's taxonomy of learning in higher education. One of these is that although students might find it challenging to understand exactly what lecturers mean when they use the language of the taxonomy in assessment tasks or learning outcomes, it allows lecturers to mark pieces of student work and to design assessment tasks with some degree of objectivity. Here, we ought not to forget the origins of the taxonomy project as it shows us precisely what was intended from the outset in relation to student learning and the need for objectivity.

The authors of a teaching guide produced for the Center for Teaching at Vanerbilt University claim that the taxonomy has merit because it allows students to get a grasp of what the 'learning goals' of a module are and ensure that these are aligned against what the lecturer understands them to be. In other words, it mitigates against an 'impasse' in interpreting the whole point of learning certain material and engaging in activities around learning that material or being assessed on it. Overall, having clear objectives and goals for learning enables lecturers to

plan and deliver appropriate instruction,
design valid assessment tasks and strategies,
and ensure that instruction and assessment are aligned with the objectives.
> Bloom's Taxonomy | Center for Teaching | Vanderbilt University

While the taxonomy emerged when Bloom was working as a university examiner at the University of Chicago, it is believed that he could not have envisaged the revolutionary nature of what he had produced at that time. The *Taxonomy of Education Objectives* slowly emerged when he, his collaborators and the university examiners were challenged by the distinct lack of clarity about how to come to objective decisions regarding assessments. There was no real system available which would help them to do this. So '[t]hey sought to construct a systematic method of evaluation so that professors and administrators could share insights and practices using a common language' (Bertucio 2017, 480).

Although Bloom could not have known the lasting influence his work in Chicago would eventually have on generations of educators when the project

26   Good Curriculum Design, Active Learning and Imagination

began, there is no doubting the importance of this work in HE today. To have a comprehensive way to grade student work which is universally applied across the HE environment is a way to somewhat ensure that standards are maintained and to ensure that there is a degree of transparency in how grades are awarded and decided. We know that students internalise a lot of information when they are learning – some of which might never be assessed – but there are other aspects of their learning that are most definitely measurable. This is what the taxonomy tries to achieve. It is for this reason why some scholars draw a link between the foundations of the taxonomy with the Cartesian method, that is, because it includes reliable rules which are easy to apply and enable academics to make objective judgements about standards and there, to some extent, eliminate human fallibility from the marking and assessment process.

But this is not to say that the taxonomy is the best example of how to measure everything that students learn and/or demonstrate that we have taught our students. Following the thought of Karl Jaspers, for instance, Bertucio tries to point out that the taxonomy is still only measuring what might be referred to as external or visible changes in student learning. In this sense, it sees all learning as 'tending towards activity' (Bertucio 2017, 488). Another way of expressing this might be to say that because Bloom's taxonomy focuses mainly on measuring analytic skills, it tells us very little about what might have changed in relation to a student's grasp of reality, truth or being.

A notable proponent of this view is Karl Stern, who argues that generations who studied and lived after Descartes' wake are suffering from 'alienation' (Stern 1965). In saying this, he wishes to highlight the fact that learning can become closed on to itself. It can become purely abstract – detached and evaluated solely on evaluative criteria and not in relation to perhaps experiences in reality, feelings of joy, wonder, surprise or inner knowing. At times, we can be led to believe that the examination of the task itself is elevated to the extent that the actual learning or value of what is learned itself becomes secondary.

Moreover, the joy of learning is not expressed and much rarely even talked about. This might be posed in the form of a question: 'Are we expecting students to become masters of achieving measurable learning outcomes, or are we also allowing them to develop as people, experience joy and wonder in the search for meaning and truth along the way too?' 'What about considering the kinds of values that the knowledge we are testing is instilling in our learners?' 'Is there space to enquire about this?' 'Or are we simply isolating the measurable from deep and less measurable outcomes of learning – whether intended or unintended?'

It is interesting to note that although the taxonomy includes three dimensions: (cognitive, affective and psychomotor), we hear more about the cognitive dimension than any other in HE debates and meetings these days. While this may seem logical given that the focus on reason and knowledge are key to learning, we must also not forget that 'affective' dimensions of learning can lead students – or anyone for that matter – to 'feel' a problem, to have empathy and compassion about the issues within a discipline, a problem or within society. The affective dimension of learning, for instance, is thought to have five categories that progress from 1–5, as outlined here:

1. Receiving phenomena
2. Responding to phenomena
3. Valuing
4. Organisation
5. Internalising values

The components outlined in the previous section show us that in affective learning, the dimensions help us to learn values and that this kind of learning can help us eventually to hold those values as part and parcel of who we believe we are as people. As Hamad Odhabi points out, '[the] components range from being able to receive phenomena to internalising values, which means that certain values have control over a person's behaviour for a sufficiently long time until the behaviour becomes a lifestyle for that person' (Odhabi 2007, 1127). Linked to this affective dimension which helps us to formulate and live out values that make sense to us in life is the psychomotor domain, which involves a progression from perception to 'adaptation/naturalisation'. This means that once we have mastered the cognitive domain and moved towards holding the values derived from the affective domain, we can get to a place where things come more naturally. We may find ourselves and our students reacting naturally or automatically to issues and problems, solving them with knowledge, skills and values such as empathy so that a well-rounded response is evident.

All of this shows us that we need to try to recall the other dimensions of Bloom's taxonomy as well as the cognitive, as these also help us to understand how we can support students to learn subject knowledge, master it, and apply it in the real world informed by a set of values that enable sensitive and considered solutions to emerge in complex situations, professional environments, societies and marketplaces.

In short, therefore, as much as the new lecturer will have to embrace Bloom's taxonomy as much as possible in relation to curriculum design efforts and setting standards for what should be learned in any given session, there should also still be a place for joy and wonder, asking deeper and less measurable questions about our disciplines and space to explore these together. Transforming minds is also an aspect of what higher education is all about. So, in busy schedules where learning outcomes must be met, we should also try – where possible – to include some space and time to being more imaginative with our students, allowing them to explore their own minds and who they are becoming as people studying a programme or discipline.

Constructive Alignment

All of this of course largely depends on what actually happens in the classroom where the lecturer is interacting with their students. Many lecturers, especially when they are newly appointed, are very focussed on the content and getting through all the required material that is needed for assessment that it is easy for them to forget to also remember to make the learning enjoyable for students. Sit and think about ways of engendering a sense of fascination and wonder about the subject discipline, rather than delivering sessions in which both student and lecturer simply 'silently' agree to 'get through' what is required because both parties know how much it matters to the students' future.

When we are looking at the learning outcomes or indeed considering designing the latter, we should begin with asking ourselves: 'what do students really need to know at the end of this module?' (Race 2014, 58). We can then build in activities that enable students to make sense of the assessment by actually actively engaging in an enjoyable activity that is linked to the learning outcomes. This is known as 'constructive alignment' – another term which new and existing staff need to understand and reflect upon especially when they are responsible for the design of new programmes and/or modules.

Following the well-known work of Biggs and Tang (2011), constructive alignment refers to the need to link the assessment task and the activities in our teaching practice with the learning outcomes. By so doing, it is thought that everything we do by way of teaching and preparing students for the assessment is closely aligned behind the learning outcomes. This also includes the kind of feedback that we give learners along the journey towards achieving the assessment tasks. Everything we do in a module, unit of study and/or academic programme must align against a rationale for doing it, that is, the learning outcomes. When all of the latter are aligned, we have more clarity as academics about what we are teaching and why we are teaching it. We also have a greater insight into the kinds of activities that we might ask our students to engage in so that subsequently they will also come to understand why they are being asked to do certain tasks, why it makes sense and how it will ultimately help them to achieve the learning outcomes.

Furthermore, when there is evidence of 'constructive alignment', everything we do in our teaching practice and curriculum design interacts together in a constant process of enquiry and dialogue so that we are continuously getting our students to engage with activities and learning that prepares them to be able to evidence their learning against the learning outcomes. One challenge that often crops up for those who are new to lecturing is the fact that they have not designed the module or helped in designing the programme of study that they are now part of delivering.

This 'lack of ownership' can be challenging if the design of the module shows evidence of poorly thought-out constructive alignment. Also the staff member may not have control over changing this as they are either too junior or do not feel confident enough to speak up about it. This further explains

Good Curriculum Design, Active Learning and Imagination 29

why having a good, supportive mentor to discuss such challenges with is often one of the most helpful things a new member of staff could have.

But there is more to be said here about what we can do to ensure that learning outcomes are understood by our students. Rather than constantly trying to deliver as much content as possible, we should try to think more imaginatively about designing engaging tasks for students which enable them to understand the assessment, get feedback on how they are doing, and ultimately meet the requirements of the learning outcomes. Carefully designing sessions is vital as it cuts down on the temptation to be overly focussed on delivering content to the detriment of engaging students in the process of learning in our classrooms. Less PowerPoint and more careful planning of *activities* that are constructively aligned should be a priority for academics.

Using Post-it Notes is often a good way of getting students to comment on something related to their learning. This can be done quickly to test knowledge and doesn't have to require all students speaking either. It can be a very quick knowledge test which seeks to find out if students genuinely know what they are meant to know or whether more needs to be done to get them to the required standard. Groupwork is also useful.

It is not unusual to have very able learners as well as those needing more support in the same group. Carefully crafting activities that are led by students who have understood the learning can help to facilitate a supportive peer-to-peer learning environment in which students are learning from each other. The student who knows the material very well gets the opportunity to teach others and to simultaneously develop other skills, such as leadership, for example. This kind of activity may help those who have difficulties to be more open about what exactly is proving difficult because the power dynamic between the lecturer and the student is no longer there. In short, the motivation for learning and for opening up about the challenges of learning may be easier when the leader of the group activity is a peer.

Digital apps such as Vevox and Kahoot are also great ways of finding out whether students understand what is being taught. They are quick and easy to use and can enable lecturers to test knowledge in a fun and engaging way for students. They are also very useful for gathering anonymous feedback. When students come to understand that their names will not appear on the lecturer's side of the app, they tend to be more open and honest about what they know and don't know in relation to their own learning.

But aside from these more modern, digitally enhanced techniques, there is also a need to remember what might be considered to be quite old-fashioned now but which still makes a difference to how students interpret what matters in the classroom, that is: how we use *our voices* in the classroom.

If we come across as timid or uncertain when we are explaining something, students pick up on this immediately. Confidence engenders more confidence. Consequently, it is essential that students do not arrive at the belief that any lecturer is 'guessing' what is important in their learning but that the lecturer

30 Good Curriculum Design, Active Learning and Imagination

can be completely trusted to support them and to be competent getting them to where they wish to be on their learning journey. Race (2014) lists nine aspects that we should keep in mind when communicating with our learners:

- Tone of voice
- Emphasis on particular words
- The power of pause in a sentence or phrase
- Speed of speech
- Repetition, when something is important enough to hear again and again
- Eye contact
- Facial expression
- Body language
- Gesture

(Race 2014, 56)

One might also wish to add 'energy' and 'excitement' here. Students pick up on and sense it when we are bored with the material that we are teaching. Being enthusiastic about what matters in a lecture engenders more interest from students as they can become inspired by our passion for our subject and by the ways in which we teach it. How you come across really matters.

A further insight that is relevant here is related to Bloxham and Boyd's (2007) work on 'tacit knowledge' – a concept referred to in Chapter 1. As lecturers in a particular field of study, we already have what might be called 'insider's knowledge' into what matters in our discipline or in our curriculum. Tacit knowledge is sometimes referred to as the 'hidden knowledge' that lecturers have about assessment (Bloxham and Boyd 2007, 68). Our tone of voice and the activities we ask students to in class should convey to students what might otherwise be 'hidden' or unclear about assessment tasks. And giving them the clear rationale for class activities should also help towards enabling every student to become assessment literate. Where the lecturer places the 'stress' on aspects of learning really matters as it can help the students to unlock for themselves what is important.

When we think about learning communities, we may also need to remember that we ourselves have been a beginner in this community at some point before we became proficient in the requirements and/or expectations. How therefore can we expect our students to know what an assessment task requires of them if we haven't explained it to them? We cannot expect learners to swim in the deep end when we have never taught them how to swim. Therefore, in order to fully understand what our learners need, we need to always see ourselves as being in a continuous cycle of reflection on their needs and in dialogue with them concerning what they believe their needs are. As Dweck's (2013) article 'Do you trust your ability to grow' reminds us, we need to keep in mind that we never know it all. We are in a constant cycle of questioning what we thought we knew.

Few lecturing staff would disagree about the need to understand learners, but how many opportunities are we genuinely providing for them to ask questions, to say that they don't fully understand, to gain more guidance and feedback on their learning and to feel understood, accepted, and included in the learning? Are we genuinely able to say with confidence that we know for certain that our learners feel supported? Or are we worried about giving too much power away or hearing that what we have been doing has not helped learners to achieve the learning outcomes?

Of particular significance here is the need to know our students. The demographic of a student cohort is important knowledge for lecturing staff to have to hand and to understand. We need to know whether we can assume any prior knowledge or experience of assessment, for instance. As York and Longden's important work points out, some students may become even more disadvantaged in their learning because they bring very little tacit knowledge with them prior to attending university (York and Longden 2004). In this sense, therefore, we can inadvertently perpetuate the social injustices that prevent some students from accessing higher education in the first place in the classes where those who have managed to get a place are trying to adjust and learn the 'rules of the game'. As with our conclusions in Chapter 1, values really matter in lecturing as without them we cannot be assured that staff are in a genuine dialogue with learners about what they need to be successful and to feel a sense of belonging in their learning environment. And we should see the need to demystify the assessment as a moral imperative in the HE sector as it is a key way to ensure a more level playing field between students of all backgrounds.

Some might suggest that this kind of dialogue and sense of belonging should come from personal tutoring rather than from time-poor lecturing staff who are delivering content aligned against specific learning outcomes. However, in actual fact, even the research on personal tutoring shows that students are more likely to disclose their issues to a member of the teaching staff than to staff in any other department at the university – including the Students' Union.

In 2002, Dodgson and Bolam's work showed that even if students have access to extensive sources of support on campus through professional services or the Students' Union, they are still more likely to contact their personal tutor for support more than any other person on campus (www.unis4ne.ac.uk/unew/ProjectsAdditionalFiles/wp/Retention_report.pdf.).

A key question to ask in the current context, however, is whether this research is still ringing true as regards student behaviours around accessing personal and academic support. Contemporary research on teaching and supporting students carried out in the Covid-19 context by Neurwirth et al. (2021) reminds us that, in a post-Covid context, faculty must not think that there is an option of *going back* to the way things were or going back to whatever was previously considered to be normal. The old normal may not now be appropriate to the new normal for students.

32 Good Curriculum Design, Active Learning and Imagination

As Neurwirth et al. put it, 'the mode that faculty should be in is *not resumption*, but rather *re-envisioning* and *re-imagining* the design and delivery' of all aspects of what we offer students in HE – both in relation to the curriculum, assessment and personal support (Neuwirth et al. 2021, 143). The same scholars also remind us that during Covid-19, some students did not access online support with personal tutors because of embarrassment about turning on cameras and being judged by others because of their environment or where they come from (p. 148). This sense of embarrassment is relevant universally to all students as a matter of fact. In all teaching and learning contexts, we must ensure that any signs of embarrassment about asking questions, understanding the assessment tasks, accessing support, experiences of education, talking about home environments or countries of origin, for instance, should be eliminated. Students must feel comfortable in our classrooms.

Although focussing mainly on the Bangladeshi context, the feelings that these students expressed are a signal to those working in higher education settings to always be mindful that our own assumptions and/or experiences of education, learning and assessment literacy are not always aligned against those of the students who sit in our classrooms. An openness therefore to always be willing to learn from students and their context and/or feelings about sense of belonging is an essential characteristic of making learning happen in any HE context. Again, the ethical stance taken by a lecturer concerning who they wish to be and the kind of values they wish to exhibit and make concrete in their learning contexts really make a difference in relation to student engagement and belonging in HE. In other words, values really matter.

All of this suggests that even when we consider all that is involved in ensuring that our lectures/modules and programmes are constructively aligned, we still need to focus on the kind of environments that we create and on the behaviours and values that we are exhibiting in the eyes of our learners. If they do not see themselves as belonging in our classrooms or able to approach us to ask for support, it is difficult to see how we could ever legitimately claim to be authentically supporting their learning.

Active Learning

Active learning is another concept that new lecturers will hear a lot about as they attend meetings on learning and teaching, programme committee meetings and/or conferences on teaching practice. As its name suggests, active learning involves making the activities around learning more 'active' and engaging for students. Although there are times where the traditional lecture may be appropriate, generally speaking, lecturers are encouraged to get students doing something in order to really engage them in the learning. Merely sitting listening to a lecturer is not considered best practice, and the chances are, if we adopt such an approach, students will be passive receptors or note

Good Curriculum Design, Active Learning and Imagination 33

takers. Where this happens, we have very little guarantee that they are genuinely engaged in their learning. According to the Berkley Center for Teaching and Learning (2022),

[a]ctive learning generally refers to any instructional method that engages students in the learning process beyond listening and passive note taking. Active learning approaches promote skills development and higher order thinking through activities that might include reading, writing, and/or discussion.

In this sense, it is all about student engagement and participation in their own learning.

'Doing' something related to the unit of learning or linked to the learning outcomes of a module helps students to retain the learning and engage more deeply with it. Active learning, then, can be said to move students away from being passive about the information that we want them to understand and process and/or apply towards a stance that encourages students to take more ownership of their learning and to engage in tasks linked to the learning outcomes. Some scholars also refer to the term 'metacognition' in relation to active learning as it is essentially students' ability to think about their own 'thinking' processes. They learn more about how they are actually learning and thereby gain a deeper awareness of how learning works. Groupwork that helps students to engage with the topic, polling apps, 'Think, Pair and Share' activities, case studies linked to real-life situations, concept maps, quick 'minute' papers given by students and student plenaries (where students sum up the learning in a particular session) are all examples of how we can get our students motivated and actively engaged in their learning.

Although quite dated now, the seminal work prepared by the Commission on Behavioural and Social Sciences Education National Research Council (1999) is still very relevant here. It makes it clear that active learning is aligned against the philosophical, psychological and behavioural understandings that exist about how we learn.

Humans are viewed as goal-directed agents who actively seek information. They come to formal education with a range of prior knowledge, skills, beliefs, and concepts that significantly influence what they notice about the environment and how they organize and interpret it. This, in turn, affects their abilities to remember, reason, solve problems, and acquire new knowledge.

(p. 8)

Therefore, if we do not allow our learners to be goal-orientated, active seekers of their own knowledge, then we are going against the very fabric of what humans understand learning to be about. According to the Commission

34 Good Curriculum Design, Active Learning and Imagination

on Behavioural and Social Science Education National Research Council, even young children are goal-oriented and active in relation to learning. They do not understand everything that is happening in the complex world that they are born into but instead they understand bit by bit. They seek new knowledge based on what they know already. They discover more as they need more. They grow and develop gradually through a process of active enquiry, and their brain 'gives precedence to certain kinds of information: language, basic concepts of number, physical properties, and the movement of animate and inanimate objects'. To put it in more general terms, to understand how our students learn we must understand that people construct new knowledge and understanding based on what they already know, have experience of and believe to be true (cf. Vygotsky 1962). This is known as the constructivist school of thought.

In this line of thinking, there is an acknowledgement that students come to the learning environment already knowing things about the given topic. They have some prior knowledge. They bring with them, too, a set of beliefs, understandings of concepts and experiences that have shaped their views of given subjects. Therefore, to leave the learning out of the process of acquiring more knowledge or to teach in a way that ignores the need to build on existing knowledge is to disregard a fundamental human characteristic about how we learn. Asking students, therefore, what they know about a particular topic can be helpful for the new lecturer as they seek to understand the level that students are at. Activities that draw out what students already know about a given topic helps the lecturer to see what they know and how much additional work needs to be done in order to construct new knowledge for students.

It also helps the lecturer to see whether what students know is based on bias or some kind of misinformed view of a subject, for instance. An example might include interpreting biblical texts in the case of theology students. Students whose view of the biblical texts does not include the need to interpret them from a historical perspective may not appreciate a session based around literary or historical criticism of sacred texts as they may have never heard of such an approach. Furthermore, if they see the texts as sacred and have only ever used them for worship or indeed viewed them in a more literal fashion, they may be offended at the idea of a lecturer interpreting them otherwise. In this way, then, constructivist approaches have many benefits, including keeping the session focussed on techniques that promote active learning, determining levelness of a session, as well as respecting what experiences and learning students may already have. Rather than repeating what they already know, we begin where they are at and build from there before the student is subsequently able to construct new knowledge for themselves.

Group activities and polls can help to determine what students already know, get them actively engaged in their own learning and promote an atmosphere of 'being in it together' between the lecturer and the student.

Inquiry-Based Learning

Closely linked to the active learning approaches that were discussed in the previous section is an approach to learning which also promotes active engagement with a subject or topic: inquiry-based learning. In this approach, the student is deeply involved in researching a topic and discovering various dimensions of a topic through a problem or scenario. This approach engenders a real sense of ownership around the learning on the part of the student, as well as enhancing research skills in a very practical way.

As Bill Hutchings puts it,

> EBL describes an environment in which learning is driven by a process of enquiry owned by the student. Starting with a 'scenario' and with the guidance of a facilitator, students identify their own issues and questions. They then examine the resources they need to research the topic, thereby acquiring the requisite knowledge. Knowledge so gained is more readily retained because it has been acquired by experience and in relation to a real problem.

This kind of approach really enhances the student experience, instils confidence in students as regards research skills and gives them the skills that they need always to be engaged in the lifelong quest for knowledge and understanding (What is Enquiry-Based Learning | Centre for Excellence in Enquiry-Based Learning (The University of Manchester)).

Developing new knowledge is not just something that is the remit of a student while they are at university. Rather, the skills that we learn at university should equip all of us to be continuously in a process of discovery about our work, who we are, and the skills we need to grow and to develop in life. The process is ongoing. As Hutchings tells us, '[i]t is essential that our students are educated for knowledge creation, lifelong learning and leadership. They will take on leading roles in their future environments directing change, asking important questions, solving problems and developing new knowledge'. In this sense, then, it is clear that how we teach our students and the methods we employ in our classrooms for learning have a direct link to the employability skills needed to be a lifelong learner in a particular field. If we think about it deeply: 'why would we stop learning if we want to progress in our careers and understand more or create new knowledge related to what we do every day?' Learning never ends. Therefore, the more tools we can give our students to use post-university, the better able to really lay claim to being employability focussed universities we will be.

But the advantages of inquiry-based learning are not simply limited to employability. A study on inquiry-based learning carried out by researchers from Canada, USA, New Zealand and Ireland showed that there were additional benefits to enquiry-based learning as long as academics were willing to

36 Good Curriculum Design, Active Learning and Imagination

let students lead, to be vulnerable in times when students know more and to trust the process (Archer-Kuhn and MacKinnon 2020).

The first of these benefits is that IBL engenders trust between the lecturer and the student. Because the power dynamic shifts from the lecturer being in charge of everything in the classroom to an environment where the student is researching scenarios or issues, nobody has all the answers as such. The learning will take place if and when both parties trust the process. The lecturer has to trust that the student will do the work and the student has to trust the method itself in comparison to the value of the traditional lecture, for instance. Put simply, both parties have to ' "get comfortable" with "being uncomfortable" given the likelihood of making mistakes, taking wrong turns and encountering "speedbumps" along the IBL journey' (Archer-Kuhn and MacKinnon 2020, 2). Trust therefore is an essential component of all that is involved in getting the best results for student learning using IBL.

A further benefit of IBL derived from Kuhn and MacKinnon's study is that it creates an 'environment of negotiated mutuality'. In other words, we take a risk when we use IBL with our students. We risk that a student for instance finds a resource or new knowledge that challenges what we even knew about a topic or forces academics to admit that they do not know the answer to some question. We are extremely vulnerable in front of our students when this happens. But if the environment is already one of trust, students and staff understand that no single person knows everything and that sometimes in learning we have to be humble about what we know or, in the case of IBL, what we may not know but have to learn from students. Academics have to allow themselves to 'get it wrong' or to show vulnerability in front of students here.

Other benefits that are brought about from IBL include a greater sense of trust between the students themselves and the creation of a space where everyone is valued and respected for what they say and in which no single person is judged when they make a mistake (Archer-Kuhn and MacKinnon 2020, 6). These skills of trust in what might be potentially vulnerable contexts are also transferrable to the workplace and to working in teams. Clearly the benefits of IBL are manifold so long as we can give ourselves the 'permission to let go' of the power and share the learning environment respectfully with our students.

Innovation, Imagination and Creativity in QA-Driven Environments

This 'letting go' of power in the classrooms can lead to greater creativity and to shared ways of learning that are negotiated between the lecturer and the student. Being imaginative is a crucial part of delivering high-quality activities that support student learning aligned against the learning outcomes as these activities give students a compass for the assessment tasks as well as for future learning too. In philosophical circles, the concept of imagination is

Good Curriculum Design, Active Learning and Imagination 37

often discussed and debated. In the field of learning and teaching there is also debate as to whether imagination refers to 'playfulness' or 'imagining' the world in order to 're-imagine' how it might be better. Whichever way one chooses to interpret the role of imagination in HE, it has a vital role to play.

Recall what we said earlier (in Chapter 1) about the employability agenda. Programmes of study are needed in order to teach skills. But beyond that, they are also needed for the formation of graduates who can think critically, see a problem or the world differently and work to make changes to solve that problem and bring about societal change. Imaginative graduates are therefore very attractive to any company that may be seeking to recruit individuals who can come up with creative solutions to old or long-standing problems.

If we take Moira Von Wright's interpretation of imagination, we can clearly see the significance of imagination in the world of work and education more generally:

> Imagination [she says] is the mental ability to visualize what may lie beyond the immediate situation and to 'see' things that are not present. It is a central element of meaning creation in education – in the relationship between mental pictures and reality, between humans and the outside world, and between past and the future. Imagination is a way of seeing, a happening in the here and now.
>
> (Von Wright 2021)

Although the term itself cannot really be tied down to a single definition, it is used in a variety of ways in education. Some use the term to refer to a kind of playfulness or fantasizing about ideas or ways of interpreting the world and/or a problem, for instance. Other schools of thought or philosophical thinkers, however, give the role of imagination a pivotal one as they believe it is paramount to making the world a better place and ensuring that old, outdated models of thinking are challenged. This 'questioning' and 'challenging' ensures that accepted norms, approaches, schools of thought are revised and forced through a kind of 'litmus test' so that they continue to serve humanity positively rather than perpetuating prejudicial views, discriminatory stances in relation to the world and/or immoral behaviours.

Von Wright's work is useful for underlining the significance of this point here too. She claims that: '[t]he socially and politically emancipating dimension of imagination has been emphasized, as has its moral significance and relation to self-formation and education'. To truly lay claim to being an educator of any kind, it is really important to recognise the significance played by the role of our imaginations and that of our students. To imagine problems and solutions differently, to dream 'outside of the box', to 'envision the world anew' are all key skills of any person seeking to make a difference in their own life, their job or in society as a whole. In order to change reality or a problem, we must almost 'dream it differently' first before we can concretely take the steps to bringing it about in the real world. Consider the entrepreneur who finally becomes recognised for their invention or model of business that is novel and financially rewarding. What led to this innovation in the first place? Being ready to 'live' and 'create' imaginative solutions, to change the status quo, or to even bring about a new commitment 'to change . . . habits when former ways of thinking prove untenable for moral and ethical reasons' (Von Wright 2021) shows how education can be utterly transformative when it is approached with vision and limitless imagination about what is possible.

Here we can clearly see that if we are to teach to transform lives, imagination is key. With the fostering of imagination comes the freedom and confidence to begin to question the world as it stands, to adopt a critical perspective particularly of the status quo that may be immoral or perpetuating limiting circumstances in any environment. To think as an imaginative person is to be continuously in a cycle of learning, questioning, accepting, and then questioning again. This continuous cycle is needed so that our ideas and ways of living, learning and working do not keep perpetuating the past mistakes that we know do not work or which perpetuate injustice in any form.

When we apply this thinking to the learning and teaching context in HE, for instance, we are subsequently prompted to see that cultivating the imagination of our students is paramount if they are to be lifelong learners, confident that they can question and see the world differently, create the future and then reflect again and again to ensure and to determine whether the answers and indeed the questions need to change.

This idea of being in a consistent cycle of questioning and questioning again is often known as the 'hermeneutics of suspicion'. A key proponent of this line of thinking was the much-loved French philosopher Paul Ricoeur. Ricoeur was known for his reluctance to see phenomena in merely contrasting terms. So he often sought to look at seemingly opposing terms or phenomena as being in a constant cycle of questioning and requestioning in order to create new meaning. Speaking about the identity of a person, Ricoeur argued that this can only be understood through the use of story as our identity is not static; it is ever changing as we grow and experience new things in our lives. So, for instance, we can come to recognise someone as being kind, caring or charitable, but this is always open to change and development. Character and self-identity, for him, are fragile concepts, which means that although our character could be constant, it can still 'include change, mutability, within the cohesion of one lifetime' (Ricoeur 1985, 246). The examined life which Aristotle spoke of is a life that has been reflected upon, engaged with imaginatively over and over again so that the best version of the self at that given moment can emerge.

But where does all of this link with learning in higher education? Often in HE settings, we hear academics complaining about the restrictions of the

Good Curriculum Design, Active Learning and Imagination   39

quality assurance procedures that accompany periodic reviews and (formerly) QAA audits that include teaching or curriculum reviews or validations, for instance. Most university quality assurance departments will have specific guidelines about learning outcomes, the layout and design of module and/or programmes as well as assessments. Most academics enjoy these aspects of their job less than teaching and doing research, but the fact remains that they are an integral part of what we need to do to ensure our programmes are quality assured and accompanied by robust processes and procedures around assessment, appeals, resits, programme modifications etc.

Given that these processes are expectations of HE regulatory bodies, such as the OfS, they are fixed, static and not subject to change by individuals at the university. But having said that, academics still need to uphold the standards inherent in their subject disciplines and teach and assess student work in imaginative and progressive ways that are fit-for-purpose for a particular discipline or subject area. In this sense, therefore, there might be a perceived tension between that which is fixed about curriculum design, requirements or regulatory obligations and the desire of any engaged lecturer who wishes to innovate as much as possible in their teaching, module/curriculum design and assessment tasks.

But these two do not have to be at odds. It is important to remember that for example even the QAA subject benchmarks do not block creativity or critical/imaginative thinking; rather, they endorse and encourage it. This means that we are called as academics to remain creative in our teaching endeavours and in our design of programmes while adhering to those regulatory, institutional norms or guidelines that are fixed and unchangeable for the time being. But it is within this very tension that the creativity needs to be considered. QA and imaginative approaches are not actually at odds. The QA processes should protect quality and ensure robust checks and balances and transparency around assessment and learning outcomes while the actual design ideas and assessment choices should always be the result of a creative quest by the lecturer to find the most innovative and progressive ways of engaging students in learning whilst preparing them for the world of work and lifelong learning.

This is similar to the philosophical work of Ricoeur again here as (when speaking about tradition) he does not juxtapose the concepts of respecting tradition or norms which may be fixed with imagination and that which is in a state of flux and/or changing because it includes imagination and interrogation of what might be considered 'the norm.' Influenced largely by the works of Gadamer and Habermas, Ricoeur is critical of the idea that history is a static concept and that what is learned from history has to be received by us without question. Instead, he argues that nothing that is fixed is mediated to us as static. Even history itself should be understood as

> an open-ended, incomplete, imperfect mediation; namely, the network of interweaving perspectives of the expectation of the future, the reception of

the past, and experience of the present, with no *Aufhebung* into a totality where reason in history and its reality would coincide.

(Ricoeur 1988, 207)

Anything therefore which is made or constructed in the past is not fixed or done forever. We are still in the process of making it. Everything in this sense that might be considered as 'the norm' or set in stone in education, for instance, is never finished. It is rather part of a constant process of interpretation, dialogue and critique. In order to do this well, we need also to be imaginative and to dare to question how we can construct the best possible programmes within a given structure or set of norms or national standards that are deemed to be set. Deep reflection on the parts of curriculum design that we may think are 'set in stone' should therefore reveal that we have more scope for creativity than we think. We should see curriculum design and QA processes therefore as being in a creative relationship where one interrogates the other with the view to producing the best quality and creative programmes of study that will equip our students to be the best graduates in a given field that they can be.

Reframing the relationship between QA processes, teaching and curriculum design with the help of a Ricoeurian hermeneutic should help the new academic to adopt a new narrative around the importance of QA and to view its requirements as an invitation to be creative rather than as something to become discouraged about or limiting. Creativity is always encouraged by everyone in the academy despite the fact that, at times, it might be difficult to see where this might fit into a highly regulated system. Nevertheless, we must be able to find this. For all the challenges that it may have presented to universities recently, the new TEF – with its focus on 'enhancement' of teaching and the student experience – is a key way for us to see whether we are already in the cycle of creativity in relation to finding new ways of supporting students and teaching more generally. Meeting the requirements should not seem like such a burden for academic programmes if we are already in the cycle of creativity within the set framework of regulations. The activities that matter should already be happening as they are borne out of that commitment that academics already have towards teaching enhancement.

Seeing the regulations that are fixed as being in dialogue with that which is not fixed should enable us to get thinking again about how we can be creative for our students in every instance. We owe them that much. After all, how just would it be if we were expecting our students to be creative thinkers and to demonstrate this to us daily and in more measurable ways in assessment tasks if we have given up on the possibility of being imaginative and creative? The call to creativity therefore should always be in the mind of the academic that loves learning and wants to pass this on to their students.

Bibliography

Active Learning | Center for Teaching & Learning. www.berkeley.edu (accessed 13/06/2022).

Adams Nancy E. 2015. "Bloom's Taxonomy of Cognitive Learning Objectives." *Journal of Med Lib Association* 103/3: 152–154.

Archer-Kuhn, B. & Stacey MacKinnon. 2020. "Inquiry-Based Learning in Higher Education: A Pedagogy of Trust." *Journal of Education and Training Studies* 8/9: 1–14.

Armstrong, P. 2010. *Bloom's Taxonomy.* New York: Vanderbilt University Center for Teaching (accessed 11/03/2023).

Bell, L., H. Stevenson & M. Neary. 2009. *The Future of Higher Education: Policy, Pedagogy and the Student Experience.* London: Bloomsbury PLC. ProQuest Ebook Central (accessed 15/09/202).

Bertucio, Brett. 2017. "The Cartesian Heritage of Bloom's Taxonomy." *Studies in the Philosophy of Education* 36: 477–497.

Biggs, J. & C. Tang. 2011. *Teaching for Quality Learning at University: What the Student Does.* Maidenhead: Open University Press, SRHE, 4th edn.

Bloxham, S. & P. Boyd. 2007. *Developing Effective Assessment in Higher Education: A Practical Guide.* Berkshire: McGraw Hill Open University.

Commission on Behavioural and Social Sciences and Education National Research Council. 2002. *How People Learn: Brain, Mind, Experience and School.* Washington, DC: National Academy Press.

Descartes, René. 1897–1913. *Oeuvres de Descartes,* ed. Charles Adam & Paul Tannery. Paris: Cerf, Reprint, Paris; Vrin, 1996.

Dodgson, R. & H. Bolam. 2002. *Student Retention, Support and Widening Participation in the North East of England.* Regional Widening Participation Project, Sunderland, Universities for the North East of England. www.unis4ne.ac.uk/unew/ProjectsAdditionalFiles/wp/Retention_report.pdf.

Dweck, C. 2013. 'Do You Trust Your Ability to Grow?' (Interview, 27/09/2013). *Nilofer Merchant* (accessed 29/12/22021).

Gershon, Mike. 2018. *How to Use Bloom's Taxonomy in the Classroom: The Complete Guide.* West Palm Beach: Learning Sciences.

Hutchings, Bill. *What Is Enquiry-Based Learning?* Manchester: Center for Excellence in Enquiry-Based Learning, University of Manchester (accessed 13/06/2022).

National Research Council. 1999. *How People Learn: Bridging Research and Practice.* Washington, DC: The National Academies Press. https://doi.org/10.17226/9457.

Neuwirth, L., Svetlana Jović & B. Runi Mukherji. 2021. "Reimagining Higher Education During and Post-Covid-19: Challenges and Opportunities." *Journal of Adult and Continuing Education* 27/2: 141–156.

Odhabi, Hamad. 2007. "Investigating the Impact on Students' Learning Using Bloom's Learning Taxonomy." *British Journal of Educational Technology* 38/6: 1126–1131.

Pitt, E. & Kathleen M. Quinlan. 2022. "Impacts of Higher Education Assessment and Feedback Policy and Practice on Students: A Review of the Literature 2016–2021." *Kent Academic Repository* (accessed 20/05/2023).

Race, Phil. 2014. *Making Learning Happen: A Guide for Post-Compulsory Education.* London: Sage.

Ricoeur, Paul. 1985. *Time and Narrative*, trans. Kathleen Blamey. Chicago: University of Chicago Press.
Ricoeur, Paul. 1988. *Time and Narrative*, trans. Kathleen Blamey. Chicago: University of Chicago Press.
Stern, Karl. 1965. *The Flight from Woman*. New York: Farrar, Straus and Giroux.
Von Wright, Moria. 2021. "Imagination and Education." *Education*. https://doi.org/10.1093/acrefore/9780190264093.013.1487 (accessed 19/06/2022).
Vygotsky, L. 1962. *Thought and Language*. Cambridge, MA: MIT Press.
Yorke, Mantz, and Bernard Longden. 2004. *Retention and Student Success in Higher Education*. New York: Mc-Graw Hill Education.

Chapter 3

Assessment and Feedback

A Constant Source of Empowerment Rather Than Imprisonment

Introduction

There is no understating the importance of feedback in higher education. Frequently, students tell us that they cannot understand our feedback, we're not giving them enough written feedback on assignments, or that we're not giving feedback to them in class either – while we may think that we are doing *all* of these. Feedback comes in many forms: from tutors, from assessments, from classroom activities, from peers and from employers. Frequently, however, we do not take enough time out to discuss *how* we're giving feedback in higher education and *whether* this is clearly understood, visible and obvious to our students.

Nor do we ask whether our feedback is helpful enough to enable learners to address areas for development. Oftentimes, when we release feedback with grades attached, our students simply look at the grade and skim over the feedback. They rarely look back at assessment feedback again once that module or unit of learning has been completed. But the onus is not all on the students. As a lecturing community we can, and should, be doing a lot more to ensure that the feedback which we spend hours giving to our students is actually taken up and implemented across their entire programme rather than it being locked in a Turnitin feedback box never to be looked at again.

So where to begin trying to unpick the key messages that a new academic might need to have to hand when starting in their new role in HE? Advance HE has done extensive work on summarising the best literature in the field concerning assessment practices and have compiled this into one key document entitled: 'Impacts of Higher Education Assessment and Feedback Policy and Practice on Students: A Review of the Literature 2016–2021'. It is worth summarising some of the key findings of this review. The authors not only advocate a much broader concept of what we might mean by assessment but they also suggest some innovative approaches that are worth knowing about at the start of an academic journey so that, when the opportunity for revalidation of the programme or redesign of modules comes up, the new academic is ready to innovate and is equipped with the most recent pedagogy to assist in this process.

DOI: 10.4324/9781003168430-4

44 Assessment and Feedback

Engaging With Pitt and Quinlan: 'Impacts of Higher Education Assessment and Feedback Policy and Practice on Students: A Review of the Literature 2016–2021'

Ed Pitt and Kathleen Quinlan from the Centre for the Study of Higher Education at the University of Kent state very clearly in the Advance HE commissioned literature review on assessment (2016–2021) that '[a]ssessment is much more than testing students' (p. 4). It is also more, they say, than simply telling students that they have succeeded or that they need to improve in certain areas. Rather, for Pitt and Quinlan, the best way to look at and approach assessment in higher education is to think of a 'broad conception . . . of assessment and feedback to centre student learning and prompt a rethinking of traditional views of assessment and feedback' (p. 4). Their central argument is that when we design and think about assessment, we should think as creatively as possible and 'integrate as many powerful principles as possible' into our decisions in this area of the student journey. A central quote from the report clearly demonstrates their view: '[a]uthentic assessments reflect real-world demands, are cognitively (and, potentially, emotionally and ethically) challenging, and help students learn how to judge their own performance' (p. 4).

The aim of the report is to encourage everyone who works with students in the HE sector to create more assessments where students can work together, as they would in the world of work, and to set the outcome of assessment tasks as measurable tasks which can be graded to measure achievement as well as determine how we could see that student's performance in front of other stakeholders, such as employers, for instance (Pitt and Quinlan 2022, 4). This is no easy task because oftentimes the new lecturer is very much focussed on getting the best research that they can find on a particular topic into a deliverable format for a lecture so it is easy to forget what they might also need to be doing to prepare students for life beyond university. Not all students will become academics who will contribute new knowledge to the field of study that they are in, but at the very least, they should reach a point in their educational journey where they have demonstrable graduate skills. The latter are not only expected in certain fields of work or professions but they are also indicative of a graduate's potential to become a lifelong learner who will continue to develop and apply those skills in their work.

In this sense, then, and when we move assessment away from just the testing of expert knowledge in a field of study, we get to the heart of a much broader definition which is linked to the world of work. In order to do this, we need to build in more innovative tasks into our teaching and assessment of students so that they have the relevant knowledge that we wish them to have from their programme along with the skills that will make them attractive to employers.

Traditional knowledge assessments can be improved by focussing on conceptual support, increasing students' interaction and gamification, and enriching the feedback design associated with them. The design of feedback opportunities should be built into assessment processes to offer an integrated and coordinated approach to improve student learning outcomes.

(Pitt and Quinlan 2022, 5)

Of course, none of these innovations and links with employability skills will be effective if our students do not see the value in getting feedback. Nor will it help students and if we haven't created the space in our modules to discuss feedback with them and to encourage them to come forward to us and to ask for clarity where they do not understand what we have said or written. In this sense, as has been mentioned throughout this book so far in relation to values and student learning, we must foster good working relationships with students so that the learning environment is one where a student genuinely feels empowered to ask about assessment, to say that they don't understand, and to admit that they are not assessment literate without the fear of being judged or feeling that they don't belong at university. '[L]ecturer feedback is more effective when it is part of an ongoing relationship with students, offers opportunities for dialogue between lecturers and students and among students over time' (p. 5).

We need also to think beyond the traditional written feedback on Turnitin assignments, for instance, and to embrace recorded messages, podcasts to student groups conveying generic 'dos and don'ts' of assessment and feedback, video feedback as well as (where practical) one-to-one feedback. Also, we must not underestimate how both inspiring and motivating it can be for students to see the work of their peers who were successful in a particular assignment because when students know others have done something, they sometimes feel more confident that they can and will succeed too. Knowing that someone else has done it and came at the assessment from the same standpoint and level can inspire confidence in students that they too can be successful.

Being Authentic and Assessment in HE

A helpful way of looking at assessment and whose role it is to do what within the process is to categorise assessment in the way that the Ministerial Council on Education, Employment, Training and Youth Affairs did when they talked about creating 'world -class assessment' for young people. There are three categories of assessment mentioned in the Ministerial Council's work:

Assessment for learning – enabling teachers to use information about student progress to inform their teaching.
Assessment as learning – enabling students to reflect on and monitor their own progress to inform their future learning goals.
Assessment of learning – assisting teaching to use evidence of student learning to assess student achievement against goals and standards.

(Melbourne Declaration on Educational Goals for Young Australians (curriculum.edu.au) 14–15)

46 Assessment and Feedback

Other principles on assessment for learning that are key to have in the new lecturer's portfolio of information is the need to ensure that students are 'assessment literate'. This point came up in the previous chapter. Making students feel included in HE is a key value that we should have if we are to truly say that we are supportive of student learning. But oftentimes we might believe that our own experience is of the highest and best quality and therefore is the 'measuring stick' or 'canon' for how our own students should be performing. Humility around how we did it is needed here. The key task is to keep asking students to tell us *whether they understand* the assessment and to keep providing opportunities for them to engage in activities that are centred around the learning outcomes of the module or unit of learning so that the criteria for the success are clear to every student. How we did it ourselves as students is secondary here. The students are the priority. To have a cohort of students where some know the 'rules of the game' and others do not is to fail to really embed professional values of inclusion into the heart of teaching, especially of groups who are from a widening participation demographic.

Geraldine O'Neill's (2017) work reminds us very clearly that

> [a]ssessment . . . has the potential to maximise or greatly hinder students' chances of success. In developed countries with mass higher education systems, designing fair assessment can be challenging given that staff differ in their views and experiences of assessments and students are an increasingly heterogeneous group. (p. 221)

In reality therefore this means that assessments can be *de facto* unfair if they are completely unfamiliar to students, and we should consider this in our assessment design by either ensuring a choice of assessment or ensuring that students do a practice run to ensure that they become assessment literate.

But of course, linked to ensuring that students understand the assessment is the need for us as academics to actually design assessment tasks that are clear not only to us as experts in that discipline but to those with no prior knowledge. The design of an assessment task is not to impress others with how much we know but to test a degree of knowledge that we expect a student at a particular level to know as part of their degree programme. In that sense, what should be at the forefront of our minds is the need to be clear about what we wish to measure from the point of view of subject knowledge and what skills a graduate in that particular programme needs to possess by the end of a programme. The route to doing this relies in part on the way in which we approach assessment. The key point to remember here is that we should always be designing effective learning tasks, giving guidance and feedback on performance, helping students to become confident about assessment, and encouraging them to reflect continuously on their own development. We also need to ensure that we always listen to student experience and feedback on assessment and take the steps to 'design out' the issues that O'Neill raises about injustice that can emerge through innovative assessment to groups of students who have no experience of such kinds of assessment (O'Neill 2017, 221). Just assessment cannot include unjust practice.

This is no easy task for the new academic as often they inherit modules and assessments that were designed by others and are part of the approved and validated documents so there may not be time or the impetus to get them changed to accommodate the expectations or expertise of a new member of staff. Over time, however, this should become a possibility for that new member of staff. By the time the opportunity to redesign a module or assessment task arises, he/she may also have student feedback on the assessment to add to making the case for changing a module's assessment design.

The point about new staff not being the author of the validated documents is also relevant when we are trying to set up learning activities in class that help students to understand the assessment and enhance their skills around a mode of assessment (be it essay writing, presentations or research skills, for instance). If we do not fully understand what an assessment task is asking students to do, we will not be supporting our students in understanding either. In this case, conversations with the programme leader or the author of an assessment task (if they are still a member of the academic team) are vital to enhancing the literacy levels of new academics around supporting students with assessment. After all, how can we expect to support our students with assessment if the assessments are not clear to us or we cannot ask other colleagues what they mean?

In order for everyone to be clear about the 'why?' of assessment tasks, the academic community needs to engage in creating what Pitt and McQuinlan term 'authentic assessment'. By this they mean that we must try to design assessments that are focussed around three main areas. The first of these is called 'realism'. Many scholars argue that students respond well to assessments that are focussed around real-life scenarios, real cases and real questions. Students often feel that they can see the relevance of the assessment task when they can see how it can be applied to the profession that they would like to join after graduation. Furthermore, simulation in subjects such as law, for instance, really inspires students and leads to higher levels of confidence as they can clearly see the 'why?' of that kind of assessment (Villarroel et al. 2018 cited in Pitt and Quinlan 2022, 19).

We could perhaps say here, however, that some subjects - where the employment route or graduate destination is not as clear-do not lend themselves to this kind of simulation quite as readily as others. Nevertheless, case studies that show how concepts are used and understood in various communities and groups, for instance, can also be helpful in fields of study where the graduate destination is not obvious. In disciplines such as philosophy, religious studies and ethics, for example, there may not be a clear route to a profession but case studies showing how, for instance, communities in society respond to debates about the environment, end-of-life issues, euthanasia and human dignity can

48 Assessment and Feedback

help students to engage with the application of abstract philosophical and ethical principles to particular live cases.

This kind of application leads to applied learning where students can really see why their subject matters and how it can in fact help communities to become more ethically driven or religiously literate or more aware of a particular moral issue. Although the government often labels some courses as 'low value', this needs further reflection as oftentimes these disciplines are fostering deep levels of abstract thinking which are needed to revise and re-examine problems and take a more creative approach to long-standing social problems (DFE and The Rt. Hon Damian Hinds MP 2019). The importance or value of courses should perhaps not simply be rated in terms of the salary they can lead to upon completion but also to the contribution they can make to how we see society, our social capital in the community, the values we hold and the respect we have for diverse perspectives on life that might be held by different groups, for instance. Society is more than just market economics.

Secondly, authentic assessment should offer sufficient levels of 'cognitive challenge'. When we discussed Bloom's taxonomy in Chapter 2, we learned that students should eventually be able to create new knowledge, critique basic concepts within their discipline of study and offer creative solutions to challenging problems and concepts. This is a higher order thinking that enables cognitive challenge and should be included in assessment design. '[A]pplication, problem solving and decision making' (Pitt and MCQuinlan 2021, 19) are part and parcel of this kind of authentic assessment. As academics we often say, 'I wish my students were more autonomous and self-directed'. At this point in assessment, however, students *should* now not need so much direction from us because they are fully equipped with the content, skills and confidence that they need to take up the challenge and offer new solutions, creative ideas and methods to a particular assessment task. If we are to take 'graduate-ness' seriously, assessment tasks must enable students to develop as critical thinkers and problem-solvers who are able to take

> a challenging attitude to what [they] read, hear and observe and be able to develop robust and cogent arguments of [their] own – either in writing, speaking or in making contexts and being willing to act on this, not just academically but in the 'real' world.
> (Learning Development (Plymouth University) 2012). How do staff and students define critical thinking? (ALDinHE).

These are key skills for every organisation and business – and for life itself. Of course, if we ourselves have not spent time carefully designing the activities to use in our classroom that will enable students to become assessment literate and critical thinkers who are confident about what the requirements are and feel empowered to ask for additional feedback and help from us, then we cannot justifiably complain that we are continuing to 'spoon-feed' students.

We are the ones who create the conditions and activities that will help learners to become proficient, confident and successful in the assessments we set and design. But underpinning all of this is the need for the assessment, at the very point of design, to be clear, carefully crafted and innovative enough to allow for cognitive challenge.

Lastly, for assessments to be considered 'authentic', they must develop students' evaluative judgement through 'transparency of criteria and opportunities for feedback' (Pitt and McQuinlan 2021, 19). In other words, nothing should be hidden or enigmatic about the assessment. Students should know how to measure their own performance, understand the requirements of the assessment and be clear about why this makes sense as part of their programme of study or module. Knowing what the benchmark for achievement in anything we take on in life is always helpful as it tells us how much we need to improve and grow in order to get to the finish line. And it is important for social change and social mobility in education that everyone knows where this 'finish line is' (HEFCE 2002).

Once again here, we are brought back to the significance of values that need to be embedded into our practice. If we do not create spaces and opportunities in our classrooms to facilitate the demystifying of assessment tasks that is greatly needed from the student perspective, then we are perpetuating the structures and approaches in HE which keep certain students ahead (because they learn the rules of the game elsewhere) of those who are often not networked enough to have anyone else to offer guidance other than their lecturer. In other words, we become agents of further exclusion rather than inclusion – part of the problem rather than the solution. Social capital can really matter in student learning, achievement and overall success in HE.

Assessment, Fairness to All and Being Values-Driven as Academics

Put simply, therefore, fairness really matters. We must remember that for some of our students the lecturer is the most networked and educated person that they know personally so they rely on this person engaging effectively with sector leading pedagogical information concerning what works with students to help them to succeed. Other students can get help at home, from their friends or their family on the 'how to?' of higher education. But when one is the first from a family to enter into the academy, this network of knowledge is not readily accessible in the same way. This of course is a societal issue which is not for the lecturer to solve. But an understanding and awareness of the need to see assessment literacy as the right of all students should prompt us to ensure that all students are 'in the know' about assessment requirements. As the title of this chapter suggests, we must see assessment as an opportunity for empowerment, not imprisonment.

A further factor that we often hear the more seasoned academics talking about is the fact that 'our students cannot write!' This is indeed an issue where

50 Assessment and Feedback

often grammar and discussions about how to write academically are often believed to be the remit of a skills team or a learning hub at university campuses and therefore not considered to be the job of the expert lecturer who teaches the curriculum.

Here there is a fine line to be drawn between students being supported and whose job it is to ensure that students have all the skills that they need to progress in their studies. Lecturing staff are well placed to talk about how to write as most of them have done dissertations and higher degrees which are assessed largely through a written thesis. To say that the job of helping students to write is just for skills teams and other support staff is to fail to offer help to our students, many of whom need help to 'adjust to the demands of writing at university' (Bloxham and Boyd 2007, 66). It *is* the job of the academic to facilitate classes and seminars which may also include input from skills teams and other departments but which are focussed around inducting students into what might be called an 'assessment community' (Bloxham and Boyd 2007, 66). Again, here, the academic needs to explain the rules of the game to all students to avoid any imbalance of assessment literacy, competence and understanding emerging in the classroom. And furthermore, even if it is someone else's role to show them how to write and to correct their grammar, etc, it is without a doubt the academic's job to engage in efforts that 'prepare students for assessment and help them perceive the meaning of assignments and the standards expected of them' (Bloxham and Boyd 2007, 66).

In a world where academics are being stretched to meet targets and expectations in both teaching and research, it is perhaps easy to get caught up in a cycle that pushes responsibility for assessment literacy away from their role to someone else's. But students listen to academics more than any other group on the campus and need help from them to move from being novices in assessment to becoming confident, fully competent members of the assessment community that is typical of their subject discipline. Generic guidance about writing is one thing but integration into the assessment community is quite another, and it is the job of the academic to take this on and make it happen for all students in their classes (Cf. Lave and Wenger 1991; Fuller et al. 2005).

It is clear therefore that while help with academic literacy can be shared across departments, there is a need for academics to engage in the subject-specific explanations for students that will enable them to move into a much deeper understanding of what assessment is all about. Students should know how they will be measured and where they need to improve needs to have a context so that students know what they are meant to be aiming for and how it will be measured. We can only speculate about whether this will lead to more students spending time reading our feedback, but at the very least, for those who do, it should make more sense.

It is critical to engage in techniques around 'assignment unpacking' for all students but especially for those students who are engaged in interdisciplinary programmes or joint honours programmes as there may well be subject-specific knowledge about assessments that students need to be able to differentiate depending on which assessment they are completing and for which subject. And furthermore, we must always be meeting as programme teams to ensure that as academics we understand the published criteria for assessment ourselves in case any tutor's view is contradicting the view of other tutors on the programme or the published criteria. Everyone needs to be on the same page regarding assessment requirements across the programme. Poor communication across programme teams should not be an excuse for students being confused about assessment requirements. Crook et al.'s work (2006) is a really helpful reminder here for us to avoid placing varying degrees of importance on certain assessment tasks just because it is our own preference and not what is published in the validated documents or in the module handbooks given to students.

We should try to remember the assessment and the associated feedback are not about us as academics but about the students and their ability to decode their meaning and demonstrate achievement against validated expectations. It's all about students and their learning. And we as academics are in service of that process of learning and student development.

We should be mindful of the words of Marcia Mentkowsky in the foreword to Merry, Price, Carless and Tara's book on *Reconceptualising Feedback in Higher Education*. She says that

> [f]eedback is a moral act and that is why it is an essential part of humane teaching and assessment. My colleague, Georgine Loacker, has reminded me often that the act of assessment is derived from the Latin word *assidere*, meaning to 'sit down beside'. Thus, assessing means, literally and figuratively, to sit with learners and provide our best efforts at feedback.
>
> (Marcia Mentkowski, foreword, 2013).

Also linked here is what might be referred to as our 'hobby horses' as academics. Some of us want to see particular perspectives being expressed by our students, and we get quite disappointed when we don't see these – as, after all, we mentioned them in class. We must try to move away from any ego-driven perspectives and focus on the design of the assessment, the validated and agreed assessment criteria and be as open-minded as possible when reading students' work. If we are more open-minded as to what their perspectives may be, and we convey this in class, we may engender a greater sense of creativity within our students who will know that they are not writing their assessment for a particular tutor or expected in assessments to follow particular perspectives or schools of thought and exclude others. Assessment is not about catering for the particular preferences of tutors but about the laid-out and agreed-upon criteria for student assessment.

Focusing less on preparing students to write what 'we' want them to will allow us to focus more on ensuring that everyone in our classes is on a level

52 Assessment and Feedback

playing field regarding the interpretation and expectations of the assessment tasks. In this way, our classrooms can really become places where the social justice issues that exist in society can be minimised and replaced by an environment where there is a shared understanding of tasks and equal opportunity given to succeed in assessments created for everyone who is engaged and submitting work. Academics should be 'values-driven' in this regard because as the Human Rights Careers website reminds us when the 'education system isn't committed to providing equal opportunities and privileges, it negatively impacts a society both culturally and economically' (Human Rights Careers, What is Social Justice in Education? | Human Rights Careers). And who would genuinely want to be complicit in that and call themselves an educator?

Religion, Belief and Assessment: Valuing Who Students Are

Linked to the need to have inclusive values and respect for who our students are at assessment time is the need to respect and consider the religious beliefs of our students. At times we might assume that this kind of personal affiliation is a private affair and that it is no business of the university to get involved in such matters. Nevertheless, it is important that we consider any adjustments to assessment arrangements that might disadvantage our students from achieving their best or arrangements that would somehow put them in a difficult position. As Vanessa David and Ethan Sykes (2013) point out, '[a]ll students should be shown that their religion is important and is valued in the university community' (p. 9). For some staff and students, faith matters on campus, and there needs to be relevant adjustments made to accommodate the needs of students – and staff - who fall into what might be called the 'faith- group.'

When students are fasting, for instance, or celebrating religious festivities that clash with academic commitments around assessment in particular, academic staff need to ensure that they know how to respond to students when they mention these commitments to them. They must not automatically assume that the student can actually choose not to engage in their religious worship or festivities and that they can or should prioritise their studies at every cost. Rather, there should be more of what might be termed 'religious literacy' in the ways in which institutions manage and roll out assessments, deadlines and examinations. The academic calendar should be thought through very carefully, both institutionally and at programme level, to ensure that any adjustments that might need to be made in light of religious 'seasons' can be made before the event itself and students find themselves having to complain or question the suitability of the chosen dates.

If we are to lay claim to be providing inclusive learning and environments in HE where all students are respected, valued and included in the teaching in classrooms but also in the assessment timings and schedules, then we must consider factors such as religious belief in our arrangements and planning. We should also note that some religious traditions have already written extensively about how their educational settings are run and how they provide care and support for students of faith. They even cite benefits of having students of faith on campus as their values and beliefs can often be harnessed in these colleges and promote a sense of community on campus where values such as honesty, integrity, community and responsibility can be promoted (Peck 2019). Where this is not happening, however, students do notice as it affects their student experience.

Although of course it may be difficult to always move classes and/or to even cancel classes to accommodate students who are engaged in prayer, for instance – perhaps because of the length of time that the academic calendar is scheduled for – lecturing staff and institutions should nevertheless be able to make adjustments for times when students are fasting, needing to be absent because of prayer and/or may be expected to do exams when they have reduced energy levels.

Providing the conditions for assessment where everyone has a fair opportunity and chance of success, as pointed out earlier, should be a key priority for any lecturer in HE, but many of us are not literate enough to consider how religious belief might affect assessment submission or participation and performance at exam time. We need, however, to be mindful of this. And if we are not doing it yet, we need to begin to do it. Knowing our students well allows us to know and understand their needs and to make arrangements that will enable them to be given the same opportunity for success as their peers.

One way to ensure that we are being inclusive around assessment is to engage in 'advance planning'. We can do this by consulting our students ahead of assessment, for instance, to find out if deadlines for assessments clash with religious observance or whether the time of submission or an exam is likely to be during a time when students are fasting.

We need to think ahead and consult with 'all' students – including our students of faith – if we are to make an authentic claim about universities being places of inclusivity and respect for all. But in reality, as the Think Tank Theos points out, 'much of the concern about universities, particularly when it comes to religion or belief issues, is based on assumption and rumour rather than evidence' (Having faith in universities: what life is really like for students of religion or belief – Theos Think Tank – Understanding faith. Enriching society).

Sometimes universities can be guilty of assuming that all is well because the students haven't raised it as an issue, but 'not hearing about something from students' is not a good enough reason not to plan and avoid the temptation to be purely reactive when a student complains about the lack of inclusivity as regards their religious observance or faith.

Religious observance should be discussed when planning the assessment calendar as well as any relevant data on the numbers of students that may be affected by a decision to schedule an examination during Ramadan, for instance. In order to mitigate any decisions impacting negatively on students

54 Assessment and Feedback

who may be observing a religious obligation, possible approaches could include the following:

1. Consulting with students or showing them a draft timetable for comment so that they can feedback to tutors about the suitability of exam dates and teaching schedules during periods of fasting [. . .].
2. Asking personal tutors to find out from students if they feel fully included and respected on campus as regards religious observance - where relevant.
3. Being clear about whether students are exempt from attending classes at certain times of the day so that they can pray and then return to class afterwards.
4. Letting students know where to access help and support.

It is widely known that the faith societies on campus provide a much-needed welcome space that combats loneliness and isolation that some students feel starting university. Conducted in collaboration with Dr Kristin Aune from the Centre for Trust, Peace and Social Relations at Coventry University, the Theos Think Tank's research on six universities showed clearly that faith societies on campuses acted as places where students could access additional 'pastoral and spiritual support. Leaders in these societies sometimes act as informal chaplains, acting as mentors and providing a listening ear to other students facing problems' (Having faith in universities: what life is really like for students of religion or belief – Theos Think Tank – Understanding faith. Enriching society).

But a key question that university lecturers and management need to ask has to do with whether we really know what kinds of pastoral support students are asking for from the faith societies. Is it about assessment, teaching, fairness and equity or other issues? We could fall into a complacency about understanding the student experience around assessment and learning (and thinking it is satisfactory), when, in fact, the reality is that other services and societies on campus are filling the need for students.

A further point might also be made for subjects where religious traditions are actually being examined as part of the assessment. We need always to ensure that trained colleagues have set these examinations and that they are sufficiently mapped against the relevant subject benchmarks for the programme of study and that they encourage critical reflection while being respectful of all traditions.

As the QAA Subject Benchmarks for Theology and Religious Studies 2022 tell us:

> Courses within the TRS area are designed to enable a wide range of students . . . to realise their potential and to succeed. These courses foster an environment in which all students have a sense of belonging, and are free to engage in critical dialogue, exploring, challenging, critiquing . . . deconstructing.
>
> (section 1.22, pp. 5–6)

The benchmarks for these disciplines also make it clear that where a religious mission or foundation is acknowledged by a particular university, the academic study of TRS-related subjects still permits dialogue, critique and evaluation (section 1.22, pp. 5–6). Although some may think programmes such as Theology and Religious Studies are 'low value' courses, the skills that are developed on such programmes are vital if we are to provide inclusive education and inclusive assessment that considers everyone's culture and faith tradition as well as working environments where people can dialogue and debate about values and what is significant for the common good without any one party feeling misunderstood, disrespected or excluded. It might be time for those who are experts in these disciplines to guide our thinking in HE a little more around inclusive pedagogy and inclusive assessment and teaching practices – especially in relation to religion and belief. And this needs to be done before these programmes disappear from university portfolios altogether.

Assessment and Giving Feedback: Tailoring Our Approach With Jisc

A further consideration which needs to be factored into any approach to student assessment and feedback is the need to be mindful of the kinds of feedback we are giving in relation to the kinds of assessments that have been set for students. Jisc produced a helpful report on 'Effective Assessment in a Digital Age' in 2010, which stipulates that receiving good feedback from lecturers 'is vital to student's learning, is their right and should be tailored to the kinds of assessment tasks that are being set' (Cf. Jisc 2020, 1–62).

Drawing on the Quality Assurance Agency for Higher Education (2006) Code of Practice for the assurance of academic quality and standards in HE (section 6): 'Assessment of Students', the Jisc report makes it clear that there are four types of 'perspectives on learning'; (1) associate (2) constructivist (3) social constructivist (4) and situative. Each of these types of learning should be followed up with a specific kind of student feedback. Once again, we see here that good assessment design and having a deep understanding of the purpose and function of any given assessment task is vital if we are to tailor our feedback in the most helpful way for our learners.

For instance, if the assessment is designed from the 'associative' perspective on learning, which focuses on students getting more competent in understanding concepts and knowledge, then the feedback required should be deep. It should also demonstrate, and be based upon, discipline-specific knowledge which details the skills that students need to develop in their subject knowledge – particularly perhaps in the early stages of a programme (QAA 2006 cited in Jisc report on 'Effective Assessment in a Digital Age', p. 11).

This kind of feedback, however, will be adjusted if the assessment task is set from the point of view of the 'constructivist' view of learning, as achieving understanding and building upon ideas that the students might already have is key to this approach. In this kind of assessment, there may well be an

56 Assessment and Feedback

opportunity for students to self-assess and to engage in an interactive discovery about what they know already and how they build upon this (QAA 2006 cited in Jisc report on 'Effective Assessment in a Digital Age', p. 11).

The social constructivist model is also similar here in the sense that it involves students actively bringing out new ideas and concepts through collaborative work and discussions. In this approach, the tasks are often shared with the group, and students may also be involved in the assessment design. In this process, students receive feedback from their peers and from collaborative activities in the learning environment (QAA 2006 cited in Jisc report on 'Effective Assessment in a Digital Age', p. 11).

Finally, what the QAA calls 'situative' learning takes place in a 'community of practice', and the feedback given can come from various sources, such as real-life tasks, employers, other professionals, peers and tutors (QAA 2006 cited in Jisc report on 'Effective Assessment in a Digital Age', p. 11).

It is clear therefore that if we are to give students the best opportunity to learn, grow and develop through their assessment tasks, then as academics we need to be as clear as possible ourselves on the rationale for the assessment strategy and design across a particular programme of study. The four perspectives outlined previously can cross over and intersect with each other (Jisc 2020, 10), but their design should be clear in the minds of the academics delivering the programme. We need always to keep in mind that students have the right to know what assessments mean and to receive feedback that is appropriate for the kinds of assessments set. As Race et al. (2005) emphasise throughout their book *500 Tips on Assessment*, what we say to students in our feedback to them will affect them for the rest of their professional lives and careers, so we must take time to get it right. The need for reflection together as a community of practice is vital if we are to keep supporting our students to get into their chosen career.

All of this brings us back to values once again. Seeing students as persons who are deserving of the best education that we can give them is the key starting point. Linked to this is the need as academics for us to see ourselves as mission-driven people who work in service of our students' development with a set of values that are not focussed on what *we* want but on the practices that best support our learners and help to prepare them to be the generation of skilled graduates that we need for the future.

Using Feedback for 'High Learning' Pay Off

In this respect, therefore, all lecturers must see themselves in a continuous cycle of reflection on assessment and feedback processes and practices that will ensure that, when we give feedback, it delivers what Phil Race's report on 'Using Feedback to Help Students to Learn' calls a 'high learning payoff' for students.

Other key aspects of giving good student feedback are related to competence levels of our students. Explaining to students where they have gone wrong through feedback is known as 'conscious incompetence'. We give this type of feedback most frequently to students as we try to move learner's understanding of assessment towards a place where they know what is expected of them. Pointing out where they need to improve and mapping this against the relevant learning outcome can point students in the direction of becoming much more assessment literate and aware of expectations on assessment.

'Unconscious incompetence' is much more difficult to address, but we must, as assessors, be aware where this is happening in the student work that we are assessing. Students often don't know or understand where they are going wrong in their assessment tasks, so we have to move them away from any misconceptions that they have about their own competence towards a position where they are not assuming that they are doing something correctly when they are not. Sometimes when we do this with our students, there will be 'an element of surprise'. 'Some of the surprises will be unpleasant ones – where (for example) students had thought that they were consciously competent' (Race, HEA Report).

Finally, and this is particularly associated with mature learners, there are students who fall into a category of 'unconscious competences'. This is often where we detect that students are proficient in certain fields of study, but they don't realise that they are. Their life journey prior to accessing HE has often helped them to develop skills in time management, organisation, leadership or IT. Or they may have developed particular ways of working or skills that they take for granted but which are helpful on their programme of study. As Vailes (2017) points out, sometimes 'you don't know what you know and that you know. You do things almost automatically' (p. 178).

Where we notice that students have competencies around assessment that even they didn't realise that they had, we should acknowledge students and let them know about it. This can be esteem raising and very developmental for students when they hear about this. Letting students know what they are good at not only helps their confidence for future assessment but also with what Jackson calls their 'pre-professional identity' (Jackson 2016, 833–853). They become acutely more aware of what their personal competencies are, so they are able to articulate these more successfully in relevant interviews or employment contexts.

An important point to keep in mind is that the assessment we set and the feedback we give to our students is preparing them and enabling them to visualise who they want to be, measure what skills they already have and develop more as they progress and get work ready. This 'pre-professional identity' is shaped by how we address our students, how we communicate to them about their strengths and areas of development and ultimately how they will feel when they graduate. Often we fail to remember that across a programme of

58 Assessment and Feedback

study that is aligned against the relevant QAA Subject Benchmarks, we are ultimately getting students ready for the job market, and through assessment and feedback, we are developing the 'pre-professional identity' of each and every person in our classrooms.

We also need to keep in mind what the HEA assessment toolkit points out when it stipulates that our feedback should be given in such a way that it

> raise[s] students' consciousness of the strengths of their work . . . boosts students' confidence and self-concept regarding personal strengths and abilities, provides guidance on areas for further development of skills and enhancement of work . . . [as well as] enhancing students' own judgement, understanding of assessment criteria and ability to self-audit their own work.
>
> (HEA Feedback Toolkit 2013, 8)

These attributes (if present in our feedback) help students enormously to reflect on who they are becoming as a professional as well as a subject specialist/graduate in their chosen field of study. Far too often we mark students' work without the 'bigger picture' in mind and fail to help students understand that we are getting them employment ready. This may be more obvious in certain subjects than others, but all subject disciplines have key transferrable skills which students may have but be less aware about when they go to interviews or write cover letters. 'High learning Pay Off' feedback should always be helping students to see their progress and how well they are progressing towards their career goal.

It is also very reassuring when lecturers give positive feedback to students who are perhaps under-confident or first generation in their families to attend university. Telling students what we think they are good at is also very empowering. Our feedback as academics *should* be empowering for students as whatever we say in our feedback can help with confidence in future assignments and positively enhance how students see their own abilities to succeed. This, of course, applies to teaching too. As Holland (2003) reminds us: '[l]ecturers must create environments which foster student confidence' (p. 15). And furthermore, by providing inclusive classroom experiences combined with inclusive and empowering feedback to students on a regular basis, we can ensure that every student and their 'story has value'. In this way students are more likely to feel better about [themselves] (Tett 2000, 193).

Where students trust their lecturer and feel valued, they are more likely to trust any innovations in the teaching styles too – as well as assessments. As Kuhn and MacKinnon's work demonstrates, trust from our students is vital to their progression, willingness to engage with innovative teaching strategies and develop more skills for themselves through the activities set by tutors. Trust is vital in the student journey towards developing the necessary skills for employment and demonstrating to employers that their graduate attributes are of the highest possible standard (Cf. Archer-Kuhn and MacKinnon 2020, 1–14). Where there is no trust between the tutor and the student group, if the lecturing style changes or is seen somehow to be inconsistent with practice in other modules, students often become suspicious about standards of teaching. In relation to feedback and assessment, this also applies. If students come to believe that a tutor does not understand the assignment themselves or that their feedback is incomprehensible or unfair, trust is lost.

We must also remember that, as McDowell and Montgomery (2012) argue, our feedback is for students and not simply a mechanism to demonstrate that the university and/or programme team has

> tangible evidence that appropriate feedback mechanisms are in place on our courses. This might mean that the feedback comments tend to look back at what was done well and less well, rather than forward to future work. Consequently, students often feel unable to transfer the guidance to other pieces of work, which may seem to the student to be quite different.
>
> (p. 75)

Feeding forward to students on what they need to do next is vital for their continued success in assessment and on their programme generally. In this sense, we not only need to be providing the feedback to learners but also ensuring that our students find it useful. Consulting with them on how useful they find their assessment feedback is vital for shaping any tutor's approach to writing and giving feedback to learners. Comments that stand alone, such as 'good' or 'very good' or 'good point', may make sense to the lecturer who has set the assignment, but we need to ask ourselves constantly, 'will this feedback make sense to our learners?' If we were students, would comments like these make sense to us? Or would we still be asking 'what *was* good about this part of my assignment as opposed to other parts?'

The language used by us as tutors is vital to students feeling empowered to be able to improve rather than just feeling relieved that they 'somehow managed to get through'. Nothing should be mysterious about how they improve their performance. Lea and Street (1998)'s work reminds us of this as they underline how oftentimes the language that tutors use in their feedback is so discipline-specific and comes as second nature to the tutors rather than to students that if it is often only partially understood by students (cf. pp. 157–172).

In order therefore to genuinely bridge the gap between what students currently know and what we would like them to know or be able to do next time, it is vital that we 'feed-forward' and give them clear advice on what to improve for next time. The latter is considered to be more sustainable in relation to student learning. We might call 'feed-forward' a kind of growth-orientated feedback that leads to change over time as it projects students into the future assignments that they will do and encourages them to reflect on the skills they

60 Assessment and Feedback

need to develop in order to be more successful next time. 'While the quality of the comments [themselves] is important, the quality of the students' interaction with those comments is equally, and perhaps more, important' (Nicol 2010, 503).

We should therefore always give students the opportunity to ask questions either on a message board or an MS Teams page, where they can ask generic questions about the meaning of feedback and feed-forward. We could also (especially if we are teaching large groups) ask students to engage in an online poll which includes questions that enable them to let us know if they found our feedback helpful and whether it was clear to them how they can improve. Sometimes the safety of an online anonymous poll can give students a safe space to express their views on our feedback as well as any aspect of their learning journey or student experience.

This active engagement with our feedback should lead students towards the kind of 'sustainable feedback' that David Carless (2013) defines as: [a]ctive student participation in dialogic activities in which students generate and use feedback from peers, self or others as part of an ongoing process of developing capacities as autonomous self-regulating learners.' (Carless 2013, 113) Getting students active about learning more generally is associated with techniques for the classroom that can promote active engagement with the topic rather than passive learning on the students' part. But we must also extend our imaginations to encouraging students to be active around the feedback they receive at university. If they are involved in understanding more about their feedback, they are more likely to become more confident in their abilities to self-evaluate and appraise their own learning more competently. In research conducted with students through the NUS (National Union of Students), Bols and Wicklow (2013) discovered that, for students, being able to critique their own work is also important.

> Students [they say] should not be overly reliant on feedback from tutors. One of the key skills developed in higher education is the ability to critique, and students should be supported to be able to critique their own work and that of fellow students. Developing students' abilities to peer review and self-reflect is an important skill for future employment, as well as deepening their own learning.
>
> (p. 28)

Once again here, we are reminded that everything we do in higher education with our students is ultimately preparing them for the world of employment. So, in relation to student feedback, we should not simply think of it in terms of whether the external examiner will say it's good practice but whether it is really fit for purpose in relation to student learning, lifelong learning, student self-development and employability skills for the future.

Bridging that gap between what students actually know and what we might presume they know about assessment and feedback are two different things. Fabienne Vailes (2017) puts it very well when she says that

[w]e need first to admit to ourselves that this is happening and to acknowledge that whilst we are passionate, motivated and interested in a topic and that we fully understand and know what we talk about, our students arrive with skills and knowledge which are completely different. We also need to be empathetic, as we too were students once and we didn't know as much as we do now.

(p. 178–9)

Therefore scaffolding their learning journey is essential to their development over time across their programme of study so that they become fully assessment literate and competent to interpret our feedback in the developmental way that we have hopefully written it. They will then be able to work more independently knowing exactly what skills and further help they may need to improve and grow further with each and every assessment opportunity. In this way, students have scaffolded help to move away from what we mentioned earlier about 'unconscious incompetence' to 'conscious competence' and 'conscious incompetence' because we have highlighted this to them in our feedback.

Creating the environment where students really feel empowered about assessment and learning is key. Nothing should be hidden from students or available to some but not to others. We know from some of the research on student stress that students respond better where they genuinely feel part of a community that is supportive and a learning environment where they know and trust that their tutor is listening to them and supporting them all the way. We should try to embrace the idea that the 'university is a garden where each one of us is a flower that will contribute to the overall beauty of the composition. It will also help us to accept fully that we all have a role to play' (Vailes 2017, 166–167). In this respect, every student should know how to improve, how to learn, how to do the assessment and how to interpret feedback. Universities have a responsibility to provide this for every student.

We can take inspiration perhaps from the Oxford Brookes University 'Assessment Compact', which outlines very clearly expectations of both staff and students as regards assessment standards. It is a one-page document that spells out how the learning community at the university will approach assessment – whether as a member of the academic teaching staff or as a student studying on a particular programme. Inspired in part by Price et al.'s 2010 work on the need for us to understand feedback as a dialogic process between staff and students, the university agreed that everyone would uphold some key principles around student assessment. There are five fundamental principles

62   Assessment and Feedback

that underpin the 'Assessment Compact', and they are worth citing here for the new academic to engage with as examples of institutional approaches to good practice around student assessment.

1. Effective assessment is central to learning.
2. To be effective the relational nature of the assessment and feedback process needs to be emphasized, particularly in terms of the need for active dialogue between students and staff.
3. To be effective, assessment must be recognised as a joint responsibility between staff and students.
4. The ability to assess the work of both self and others is an essential skill for all graduates.
5. For the above tenets to be met in full, students and staff need to be 'assessment literate' and actively participate in disciplinary communities of assessment practice.

(Rust et al. 2013, 150)

Having a long-term campaign and an institutionally agreed strategy or 'compact for assessment' might not be common at every university, but it is vital for the new academic to understand how beneficial such an initiative might be. If an assessment strategy is not visible or nobody is talking about one, then new lecturers should be advised to find out what the assessment and feedback expectations are. Is 'feed-forward' expected? Who moderates? Is second marking required? Does a calibration exercise need to be arranged so that you can ensure that your feedback and marks are consistent with other colleagues who teach on the programme? It is our responsibility to find out about these expectations as we owe it to our students – whether we are new to academia or not – to ensure that their experience of feedback and assessment is consistent.

Conclusions

It is clear that assessment and feedback are crucial matters for all academics to reflect on and to be engaged in as they are not only key measures by which we can track and monitor student performance but they are also the mechanisms by which students come to know where they need to grow and develop further as they progress with their programme of study. Active engagement with students on what is working in assessment and what is not is crucial if we are to enhance their learning and ensure that they are reaching their full potential while studying at university.

As students progress on a programme of study, there should come a point in that journey where students feel competent and confident that they understand the assessment tasks, can interpret feedback and feel that they are fully assessment literate. To put it differently, there should be a point in their student journey where they are clear that they have the tools that they need to feel fully inducted into and part of the 'assessment community' and where they, like their lecturer, have the 'tacit knowledge' about assessment in their own discipline. This is not an easy task especially if we are teaching students who have no experience of HE or have nobody else to ask about what to expect or where they feel they do not belong in HE and are uncomfortable asking for help.

But as lecturers, the key to remember is that all learning is about relationship first and foremost and that where students feel comfortable with us, they are more likely to trust that they can ask questions and not be judged. If we are truly to lay claim to the much-used phrase that 'students are our partners' in learning, then we really need to show that this is not just lip service but something that we live out every day in our teaching and especially in the areas of assessment and feedback. The task is clearly ongoing.

Finally, linked to the need to treat our students as partners and to seeing education as being based on relationship is the need to respect that education involves the whole person. What is going on for students outside of our classroom can impact on learning too, so we also need to consider how academic staff can play a part in the pastoral support and guidance that students may need. This is the focus of the next chapter.

Bibliography

Advance HE. 2018. *Religion and Belief: Supporting Inclusion of Staff and Students in Higher Education and Colleges*. www.advance-he.ac.uk (accessed 19/02/2023)

Archer-Kuhn, B. & Stacey MacKinnon. 2020. "Inquiry-based Learning in Higher Education: A Pedagogy of Trust." *Journal of Education and Training Studies* 8/9: 1–14.

Benfield, Greg, Chris Rust & Margaret Price. 2010. *Proposal for an Evaluation of the Oxford Brookes University Assessment Compact (v. 1.0)*. Oxford: Oxford Centre for Staff and Learning Development & ASKe (accessed 20.07/2022).

Bloxham, S. & P. Boyd. 2007. *Developing Effective Assessment in Higher Education: A Practical Guide*. Berkshire: McGraw Hill Open University Press.

Bols, A., & Kate Wicklow. 2013. "Feedback – What Students Want." In Stephen Merry, Margaret Price, David Carless & Maddalena Taras (Eds.) *Reconceptualising Feedback in Higher Education: Developing Dialogue with Students*. London: Routledge, 19–29.

Carless, David. 2013. "Sustainable Feedback and the Development of Student Self-Evaluative Capacities." In Stephen Merry, Margaret Price, David Carless & Maddalena Taras (Eds.) *Reconceptualising Feedback in Higher Education: Developing Dialogue with Students*. London: Routledge, 113–122.

Crook, C., H. Gross & R. Dymott. 2006. "Assessment Relationships in Higher Education: The Tension of Process and Practice." *British Educational Research Journal* 32/1: 95–114.

David, Vanessa & Ethan Sykes. 2013. "Religion and Higher Education." *Parameters of Law in Student Affairs and Higher Education*. HEConcersandSolutions. Religion and Higher Education: Concerns and Solutions. www.wku.edu (accessed 27/07/2022).

64 Assessment and Feedback

Department for Education and The Rt. Hon Damian Hinds MP. 2019. "Education Secretary Calls for an End to Low-Value Degrees." *Gov.UK.* www.gov.uk (accessed 27/07/2022).

Fuller, A., H. Hodkinson, P. Hodkinson and L. Union. 2005. "Learning as Peripheral Participation in Communities of Practice: A Reassessment of Key Concepts." *Workplace Learning, British Educational Research Journal* 31/1: 49–68.

HEA Feedback Toolkit. 2013. *HEA Feedback Toolkit | Advance HE.* www.advance-he. ac.uk (accessed 14/07/2022).

HEFCE (Higher Education Funding Council for England). 2002. *Partnerships for Progression, 2002/49.* Bristol. HEFCE.

Holland, S. 2003. *Council for College and University English News.* www.cccu.ac.uk/ fileadmin/documents/0208_CCUE_News_MAR_APR.PDF.

Human Right Careers. "What Is Social Justice in Education?" *Human Rights Careers.* https://www.humanrightscareers.com/issues/what-is-social-justice-in-education/ #:~:text=At%20its%20core%2C%20social%20justice,race%2C%20gender%2C%20 and%20education (accessed 27/07/2022).

Jackson, Denise. 2016. "Developing Pre-Professional Identity in Undergraduates through Work-Integrated Learning." *Higher Education* 74: 833–853.

Jisc. 2020. "Effective Assessment in A Digital Age: A Guide to Technology-Enhanced Assessment and Feedback." www.webarchive.org.uk (accessed 13/07/2022).

Lave, J. & E. Wenger. 1991. *Situated Learning.* Cambridge: Cambridge University Press.

Lea, M.R. & B.V. Street. 1998. "Student Writing in Higher Education: An Academic Literacies Approach." *Studies in Higher Education* 23/2: 157–172.

Learning Development (Plymouth University). 2012. "A Brief Introduction to Staff and Students' Interpretations of Critical Thinking." *LearnHigher: Free Teaching and Learning Resources for Staff in Higher Education. How Do Staff and Students Define Critical Thinking? – ALDinHE* (accessed 27/07/2022).

McDowell, Sambell & L. Montgomery. 2012. *Assessment for Learning in Higher Education.* London: Taylor and Francis Group.

Merry, S., Margaret Price, David Carless & Maddalena Taras. 2013. *Reconceptualising Feedback in Higher Education.* London: Routledge.

Ministerial Council on Education, Employment, Training and Youth Affairs [MCEE-TYA]. 2008. "The Melbourne Declaration on Educational Goals for Young Australians." www.curriculum.edu.au (accessed 26/07/2022).

Nicol, D. 2010. "From Monologue to Dialogue: Improving Written Feedback Processes in Mass Higher Education." *Assessment and Evaluation in Higher Education* 35/5: 501–517.

O' Neill, Geraldine. 2017. "It's Not Fair! Students and Staff Views on the Equity of the Procedures and Outcomes of Students. Choice of Assessment Methods." *Irish Educational Studies* 36/2: 221–236.

Peck, Timothy. 2019. "A Guide to Catholic-Affiliated Universities." *CollegeVine Blog* (accessed 27/07/2022).

Pitt, E. & Kathleen Quinlan. 2022. *Impacts of Higher Education Assessment and Feedback Policy and Practice on Students: A Review of the Literature 2016–2021.* Kent Academic Repository. https://kar.kent.ac.uk/95307 (accessed 11/03/2023).

Price, M., J. Caroll, B. O'Donovan & C. Rust. 2010. "If I Was Going There I Wouldn't Start from Here: A Critical Commentary on Current Assessment Practices." *Assessment and Education in Higher Education* 36/4: 479–492.

Quality Assurance Agency for Higher Education. 2006. "Code of Practice for the Assurance of Academic Quality and Standards in Higher Education, Section 6: Assessment and of Students." https://dera.ioe.ac.uk/9713/2/COP_AOS.pdf.

Race, P. "Using Feedback to Help Students to Learn." *The Higher Education Academy. Microsoft Word – Race.doc.* www.phil-race.co.uk (accessed 13/07/2022).

Race, P., S. Brown & B. Smith. 2005. *500 Tips on Assessment.* Abingdon: Routledge-Falmer.

QAA. 2022. "Subject Benchmark Statements: Theology and Religious Studies." www.qaa.ac.uk (accessed 27/07/2022).

Rust, Chris, Margaret Price, Karen Handley, Berry O' Donovan & Jill Millar. 2013. "As Assessment Compact: Changing the Way an Institution Thinks About Assessment and Feedback." In Stephen Merry, Margaret Price, David Carless & Maddalena Taras (Eds.) *Reconceptualising Feedback in Higher Education: Developing Dialogue with Students.* London: Routledge, 147–159.

Taylor, R. 2000. "Concepts of Self-Directed Learning in HE: Reestablishing the Democratic Tradition." In J. Thompson (Ed.) *Stretching the Academy.* Leicester: NIACE, 68–79.

Tett, L. 2000. "I'm Working Class and Proud of It – Gendered Experiences of Non-Traditional Participants in Higher Education." *Gender and Education* 12/2: 183–194.

Vailes, Fabienne. 2017. *The Flourishing Student: Every Tutor's Guide to Promoting Mental Health, Well-Being and Resilience in Higher Education.* London: Practical Inspiration Publishing.

Villarroel, V., S. Bloxham, D. Bruna, C. Bruna & C. Herrera-Seda. 2018. "Authentic Assessment: Creating a Blueprint for Course Design." *Assessment and Evaluation in Higher Education* 43/5: 840–854. https://doi.org/10.1080/02602938.2017.1412396.

Chapter 4

Who Are Our Students?

The Need for Racial, Religious, Spiritual and Academic Personal Tutoring

Linking to the need to foster good relationships with students such that they will feel empowered to give us constructive feedback on our teaching and on the student experience is the need to offer good personal tutoring to students too. This can often be a big challenge when lecturers are dealing with large groups of students and are time-poor trying to meet other targets. This chapter will argue, however, that universities should devote more time to 'getting to know' students and fostering good relationships with them through the personal tutoring system because this helps students to feel a sense of belonging and security in the learning environment. Personal tutoring is often described as a key 'anchor' for students at university (Owen 2002). 'Being known' by a member of the staff team can be a powerful motivation for students not only to stay at university (if they are thinking of leaving) but provides a means of support from 'someone who has done it' that can empower students to continue their learning journey.

The chapter will also argue that lecturers at all levels of the university system need training in how to approach and deal with conversations regarding race, gender, religion, and spirituality. Again, this will require considerable investment from our universities, but it would mean that universities could make a more convincing case for being places where diversity is genuinely promoted and respected in all contexts. The work of the French philosopher Paul Ricoeur will be used to show how university lecturers need leadership that can help them to navigate the path towards providing more support for BAME students and/or students of faith. His work on diversity across the European Union will be used to show how deep our understanding of diversity and individuals needs to be to facilitate genuine inclusion.

For instance, when discussing the principles for the integration of religious believers (and their identities) into a cross-cultural context such as that of the European Union, Ricoeur argues that personal identity should be maintained but that an understanding of common principles that enable these identities to be integrated and respected in society is also important. He combines 'identity' and 'alterity' as acting in a mutually interrogative way to enable individuals to both express their belief and identity while being part of a greater

DOI: 10.4324/9781003168430-5

whole (society) – which is 'other' (See Mealey 2009, 150ff for a comprehensive summary). It is this balance between 'identity' and 'difference' that I will draw upon in this chapter to help us to see how we might be able to support students in the current diverse and complex university setting. Each student has a specific identity that is unique to them but which exists in relation to the identities of other students too. These need to coexist in harmony in the community on campus. Personal tutoring can help with all of this in order to help the student to settle in and have an anchor in a place that seems to have a massive identity and be completely alien or 'other'.

Ricoeur's work on the European Union – and his work more generally – emphasises the central importance of 'story' as a means of being oneself in the context of 'other' (Ricoeur 1990). I will attempt to show that the personal tutor is not only the 'human face' of the university (Wootton 2006) but that he/she is also the means through which the student's identity/story begins to be incorporated into the university such that the student feels their 'otherness' is accepted, thereby grounding them in the learning context. Ricoeur's stress on having 'cultural translators' (Ricoeur 1992) can be an important principle for helping us to understand our students and where they are coming from as regards their own story at university. For students this is an important function of the personal tutor: the best tutor is often the one who knows their story. And this is essential to their feeling supported and often to the choice to stay at university.

The previous chapters argued that values play a significant part in authentically supporting students in higher education. Ensuring that our classrooms are inclusive in relation to how we teach, how we explain and/or 'unpack' assignments to students and how we support our students is key to their success. Much of the literature on good teaching also emphasises the need to develop and foster good relationships with students as where there is trust, students are more likely to try new things (see Chapter 3 on enquiry-based learning).

Of course, a key part of developing trust with our students has to do with how we make them feel when they are in our classrooms, in meetings with us or interacting with us in any settings or campus events. Students observe and feel everything we do and say to them as lecturers. So the more supportive we can be towards them, the better. This is where the pastoral side of higher education comes into sharper focus. Personal tutoring is considered valuable in most higher education organisations, but how it takes place and the significance that colleagues place upon it varies across the sector. Some institutions take an 'if students need me, they know where to find me' approach, while others have quite specific, target-focussed and/or employability-based methods that are foundational to the personal tutoring support that is provided to students.

Whichever approach is taken by a university, few academics would disagree that the personal tutor is indeed a key human support system for students at university (Owen 2002). For students to know that someone at the university

68   Who Are Our Students?

knows them and/or checks in with them and shows care for their welfare and progression as students is paramount to how they feel about being at university and whether they can succeed – especially when things become challenging either academically or personally. Some recent research shows that students also appreciate the feeling of 'being in it together' with their tutor and really value that support and open door being available to them should they need it (Mealey 2023, 682).

Annabel Yale's work reminds us that personal tutoring can be described as an activity that promotes the common good at university campuses but also helps the tutor and the students to establish a 'shared understanding' of what is expected at university level education (Yale 2019, 533ff). Of course, finding the time to meet with students is often difficult for the busy and time-poor academic, but when it is done with a clear focus, purpose and mission, it can be less time-consuming and more focussed around what the student needs. As Yale rightly suggests, we need to ensure that when we meet with our students for the purpose of personal tutoring that we make that time count so that students will see it as a *quality interaction* and something worth doing and engaging with (Yale 2019). Frequently students can get disgruntled if they are being asked and/or invited to attend meetings of a pastoral nature, and they don't know what these meetings are intended for or what they should achieve.

For students who commute to campus and who have busy lives and family commitments that they juggle around their studies, the idea of meeting with a lecturer for a 'personal tutoring meeting' is simply not a priority unless it is of high value in some respect or another. A further issue that should be noted when we think about personal tutoring and its significance for students is the fact that some tutors genuinely engage with the expectations of personal tutoring as defined by their respective universities, and some do not. Where this happens across a programme team, students will eventually discover that some of their colleagues are receiving more support from the team than they are, and this dissatisfaction can have a negative impact on the student experience and their feelings around being treated equally on a programme. Other challenges have to do with an ever-expanding student cohort. Some tutors are simply unable to provide the same level of personal support to students when numbers grow on programmes, which can sometimes mean that students can feel that they are missing out on 'being known' at university in the way that other students are where the programme cohort number is much smaller.

And finally, the ever-challenging research agenda and the expectations of REF related activities often means that academics do not and often *cannot* prioritise personal tutoring - as they are trying to find ways of demonstrating impact for the REF ratings for their university. And when promotions are often geared around what might be called 'REF-ready' staff, there is no real incentive for academics to spend hours with students when it won't 'pay off' in the end. In this respect, there is often no incentive – apart from a particular individual's personal commitment to students – to do personal tutoring well.

Models of Personal Tutoring

Despite the value that some staff and students (especially those who have had an excellent experience of personal tutoring) put on personal tutoring, there seems to be a range of approaches across the sector as to what students need and debates about what is genuinely possible and realistic for staff to be able to deliver (resource-wise). Few academics would disagree that, in recent years, the disclosure of mental health needs has led to an increased need for academics to enter the world of support services and to at the very least know where to refer students if they are in distress. But this creates its own issues for the new academic as they may not have had any training around the expectations of what personal tutoring might involve let alone know whether the institution has any guidance on this, or resources that would help with signposting or indeed any training sessions that would help with understanding what the expected standard or time allocation might be.

But we have to learn what is expected of personal tutoring as this kind of 'individualised learning' is respected by many institutions. Personal tutoring seems to have its origins in the personal tutoring system that existed since the sixteenth century and was pioneered by Oxford and Cambridge (Walker 2022, 65). It acted as an 'in loco parentis' approach that was designed to help and support students to develop in every possible way – intellectually, personally and professionally. The conversational approach between the tutor and the student led to strong bonds being formed between both parties. It also had the benefit of the student learning in a trusted space where they had direct contact with both a brilliant mind and intellectual expert in their chosen field of study but also to the more human side of that person whose role it also was to look after that student as a person.

But eventually this approach was deemed to be unsustainable, and many felt that it might be both too expensive to resource and also too difficult to promise to large student groups. In recent years, however, some of the scholarship has tried to bring the significance of the personal tutor back into focus at universities. Some studies show that where a student has a good personal tutor, the student often attributes their attainment and progression at university to that tutor. Bonds are often formed that last for life, and overall the student feels as if they truly belong in the academy.

For those universities who still prioritise a version of personal tutoring, it can be difficult to know how effective it is or to measure it, but the models are diversifying now and linking to graduate skills in some cases. Generally speaking, we can see across the sector 3 main models or approaches to personal tutoring. Earwaker proposed these in 1992, and they are summarised helpfully by Walker in 2022. Walker (2022) states that

> the most common [approach to personal tutoring] is the 'pastoral'. In this approach, every student, undergraduate and postgraduate, is assigned an

academic member of staff known as a personal tutor, and it is the standard model used in the UK sector. The personal tutor is a 'normal' lecturer/academic member of staff; one who is employed as a lecturer, a senior lecturer or a professor. . . . [T]hey are tasked with the responsibility of supporting their tutees' academic and personal development, supporting their transition into university and between levels, discussing academic progress and achievement with their tutees and encouraging students to engage with opportunities offered more widely within the university.

(Walker 2022, 6)

The second most common approach to personal tutoring is the professional model. This is where students are not allocated a specific lecturer as their personal tutor, but they know that they can contact a designated office of staff who are trained personal tutors who can offer support (Walker 2022, 6ff).

The final model, which is slowly becoming much more popular in higher education settings, is that of coaching. This approach is well-known and used within the business and personal development sectors but is still largely a new concept to HE settings (Wisker et al. 2008).

It is also often used in the worlds of sport and music. In terms of sports or musical talent, coaching as a form of development is the focused application of developmental suggestions that help individuals develop their sports, musical or other skills to the best of their ability. Singers and actors, as well as those in sports, might well have a personal coach, and this practice is based on the individual coach focused on working with the individual coachee, identifying his or her skills, needs and aims, developing a coaching plan that he or she agrees to, owns, and wants to action, then working with the coachee to him or her achieve it. Coaching has a slightly different meaning and use in the business world, but it is still about matching developmental support to the individual's skills and needs.

(Wisker et al. 2008, 9)

This approach to personal tutoring is quite unique in that it is very 'hands-off', non-directive and involves conversations that enable the coachee to identify and meet goals, improve skills and develop creative solutions to problems along with behaviours around discipline and focus. What it can potentially offer the HE sector is the ability to develop key employability skills with students in readiness for the world of work along with building skills that they need – such as resilience – to complete their programme of study. Key to the process is that the coach knows and understands what kinds of questions to ask the coachee so that they can reflect on their own developmental needs and how they may need to approach specific situations or issues. Whilst some believe that there is probably not much difference between coaching and mentoring and much overlap exists between these two domains, the role of the mentor is still slightly different. The mentor is usually someone experienced in the field of work or study, but a coach can be a business coach, or someone trained in coaching methods, who may not know the field or discipline of study the coachee is in.

All of this points to the fact that HE seems to be moving towards a learning culture where individuals are expected to be able to develop the skill of *identifying their own developmental needs* and articulating these to a coach who can ask leading questions with a view to being solution focussed. This helps to move the sector away from what Guccione and Hutchinson (2021) call a 'deficit model' of development, which suggests that a person would only need or require mentoring or coaching because they are failing. Instead, it helpfully and positively shows an approach which is much more realistic in terms of career preparation and our ability to grow at every stage of learning. Everything is in a state of flux, and so the response we may need or the skill that we may require to develop at any given point is not seen as a failing but simply as an area for development to enable further growth and competency. This should lead to greater self-reliance and authenticity overall (Guccoine and Hutchinson 2021). And what better skills would we want our students and prospective graduates to develop than autonomy, responsibility and the ability to identify and work on their own developmental needs?

Challenges to Adopting a University-Wide Personal Tutoring System

Of course, while many can see the positive case that can be made for adopting a university-wide personal tutoring approach – using one, all, or a combination of the models explained previously – implementing such approaches is not without its challenges. This section will highlight some of these.

Discussing personal tutoring and its benefits and challenges for trainee nurses, Tessa E. Watts (2011) asserts that not only can it help students make the transition from college or secondary school into the HE sector but that it also has the potential to help students to take the 'leap into what may be an unknown world' – one that requires students to adapt to the world of nursing in all its forms as soon as possible (Watts 2011, 215). Personal tutoring can also help students to cope with competing demands on courses that have a very rigorous professional placement element in that the tutor can advise students on how they managed the placement themselves as students. It can be helpful for students to share experiences and stories and for the tutor to suggest where further help might be available as well as helping them to prioritise tasks (Watts 2011, 215).

This is so important in the life of any student because although no university would claim that it doesn't care for the welfare of students and whether they can juggle their family life, emotional health and well-being with their academic studies, it is often unclear exactly how much time and energy academic

72 Who Are Our Students?

staff can put into student pastoral support. Despite this, we have to see the personal tutor as being concerned with the 'whole person'. Fabienne Vailes' work makes it very clear that every person is akin to the 'head of a flower' in that it is composed of many elements (Vailes 2017, 111). And we must remember that. Each petal on a flower (to return to the metaphor that Vailes uses) represents an element of what makes up each individual and therefore includes five health concepts: 'emotional health, mental health, physical health, spiritual health, social health, and five "skills" – flexibility, openness, curiosity, resilience, and language use' (Vailes 2017, 111).

However, if universities are to cater for all these aspects and see support for students in a very holistic way and one that is informed by multiple factors and a deeper understanding of what students may need to succeed, then we need to take a real look at what challenges and barriers to achieving this might exist in the sector.

Personal Tutoring: The Barriers to Progress

One barrier to providing good personal tutoring for students that is often cited by academics is time. Competing demands means that often any new initiative – however noble – can be met with resistance or the response that academics are too time poor to fulfil what would be required. But the concerns run deeper than this, as some studies show that academics are in fact fearful of being responsible for anything other than the academic programme and students' success academically. They are fearful of making a mistake, getting it wrong with a student and/or being held accountable for saying or doing something that might later have repercussions for them. Hayman et al.'s recent study on personal tutoring with sports students at university showed that

> the breadth, severity and complexity of topics students were now wanting to discuss had escalated in recent years . . . and that staff felt 'professionally torn' as to whether to get involved in supporting students with issues that they were experiencing outside of the university. In fact, some staff tutors said they felt 'unsuitably qualified to assist' with issues around mental health and domestic issues that are quite seriously affecting students' performance and engagement.
>
> (Hayman et al. 2022, 9)

This concern is a particularly serious one in the current climate where many students are disclosing mental health–related conditions and diagnoses – some of whom will be receiving regular treatment as part of their care programme. Without sufficient training in personal tutoring, staff can feel very vulnerable when faced with a distressed student in their office. Although the response given here is often one that signals the importance/need of academics to 'sign-post' students to relevant services, the worries often persist in the minds of academics. And oftentimes they are asking for training so that they can in fact do the right thing in moments of crises.

Other research shows that where the approach to personal tutoring was embedded in the curriculum, staff mentioned the need to consider and to find ways of managing several issues. Potential challenges included the following:

- Identifying space in the curriculum for PDP and personal tutoring activities.
- Concerns that the inclusion of these activities in the main curriculum might prescribe and constrain communication between students and tutors.
- Concerns that academic roles might be perceived as outweighing wider pastoral roles.

(Stevenson 2009, 119)

A further issue that is often cited by staff about being unable to provide equitable levels of support to all students on a programme is that increasing numbers will limit the amount of time and resource available to get to know and support 'all' students. Big numbers of students can mean that only those who are confident enough to keep contacting their personal tutor to talk about their support needs will get the real benefit that a personal tutoring system can offer. This chimes very well with Neuwirth et al.'s (2021) work which shows that while all students may need and want 'security' at university, some do not access what is available because of many factors, including feeling embarrassment about talking about their issues or – where online support is provided – turning on their camera at home for fear that they will be judged in some way (p. 148).

For these reasons, and some of the others cited earlier, Janette Myers wonders whether the current personal tutoring system will fall by the wayside in the same way that residential hall wardens did. 'These roles co-existed until the decline of the role of the warden from the 1960s', but slowly the latter disappeared over time' (Myers 2008, 607). The roles share the fact that they are both concerned with supporting students beyond the classroom setting and the merely academic side of learning and teaching. They were pastoral and were a clear and visible sign that university management teams and academic teaching staff more generally understood the need to support students as they tried to adapt, integrate and achieve their potential despite any challenges that life might have put in their path. Silver's 2004 work suggests, however, that when the trend started to emerge where students were progressing from the Halls of Residence to alternative accommodation – that was often off campus – there was less of a need to retain the role of the hall warden (Silver 2004, 127). But as the literature on personal tutoring shows, the need for a personal tutor continues as students still find it difficult to make the transition from secondary school to university, or from a professional job to full-time study, and the challenges of life often make it more difficult for some students to juggle priorities and find the resilience to keep going on their programme.

74 Who Are Our Students?

Interestingly, though, for those students who have found support in their personal tutor, they are quite clear that their success at university is due in part to this relationship.

Nevertheless, the evidence of how widespread this kind of success story is can be limited, and students often claim that their experiences of personal tutoring vary a great deal. It is also not uncommon to find that one tutor on a programme gets a reputation for being the 'go to' person when students need help and a listening ear, but this 'open door' approach is not available to all students from all tutors in a consistent way. These dynamics make it difficult to make a definite case for allocating hours in the workloads of academics to doing this work when there is no real guarantee that it will be done or even done consistently for that matter. Furthermore, at a time when the cost-of-living crisis is about to hit the HE sector quite considerably, there will be a need to support students more. But the resource or the time might not be there. This plethora of demands will undoubtedly force university leadership teams to perhaps reconsider what is genuinely necessary for HEIs to support students effectively, academically and personally. A back-to-basics approach might add weight to the idea that personal tutors should be taken seriously, trained and appreciated in promotion rounds much more than they are currently – as this work lies at the heart of the support that students say they need and often do not get. In short, we need to care for our students. And we need to have this as a key value that we treasure in HE. We care for the whole person who walks into our campuses hoping for a brighter future. And this is complex work to support a person for (at least) three years, but we have to engage with what students need in order to really fulfil what we are saying education does – which is transform the lives of students. Emotional *and* intellectual well-being therefore really matter. But this is not to say that this is an easy task as, aside from the resource issue, even the definitions of well-being are complex and demanding.

Keyes (2002) argues that for any individual to have complete mental health, one has to be able to demonstrate positive functioning in three broad areas of one's life: emotional, psychological and social well-being (p. 299). Refining these categories into the aspects that are needed for a flourishing life, Keyes maintains that emotional well-being includes numerous aspects of a person's well-being that need to be evidenced in our behaviour and dispositions for us to be healthy. When we consider Keyes' list, it's quite easy to see why caring for students through personal tutoring matters so much, but it is also daunting to think that we might be asking academics to attend to some or all of these aspects without training and support. The categories include the following:

Positive affect: the person is regularly cheerful, in good spirits, happy, calm and peaceful, satisfied and full of life.
Happiness: the individual feels happiness towards past or about present life overall or in domains of life.

Life satisfaction: sense of contentment or satisfaction with past or present life overall.

Positive functioning: psychological well-being and social well-being.

Self-acceptance: positive attitude towards oneself and past life, and concedes and accepts varied aspects of self.

Personal growth: insight into one's potential, sense of development and open to challenging new experiences.

Purpose in life: has goals, beliefs that affirm sense of direction in life and feels life has purpose and meaning.

Environmental mastery: has capability to manage complex environments and can choose or create suitable environs.

Autonomy: comfortable with self-direction, has internal standards, resists unsavoury social pressures.

Positive relations with others: has warm, satisfying, trusting relationships and is capable of empathy and intimacy.

Social acceptance: positive attitude towards others while acknowledging and accepting people's complexity.

Social actualization: cares and believes that, collectively, people and society can evolve positively.

Social contribution: feels that one's life is useful to society and that one's contributions are valued by others.

Social coherence: has interest in society, feels it's intelligible, somewhat logical, predictable and meaningful.

Social integration: feels part of, and a sense of belonging to, a community, derives comfort and support from community.

(Keyes 2002, 207–222)

When the list of what constitutes the well-being of a student/individual from a psychological point of view appears before us, it quickly becomes very clear that the task of a personal tutor (if they have a remit about genuinely supporting student well-being, that is) is enormous. It is also quite understandable why some academics feel completely out of their depth with this task and often say that they need help and guidance. Wisker et al.'s 2008 work is clear that personal tutoring really matters to students in HE and that we should see it as an opportunity to provide more than just the learning and teaching experience to students.

As a personal tutor [they say], you have the opportunity to put . . . anxieties into perspective and guide the student through any initial difficulties. You can help to establish realistic expectations, encourage effective study patterns, and generally contribute to a more fulfilled student experience, by offering continuity throughout their degree.

(Wisker et al. 2008, 46)

But putting 'anxieties' into perspective may mean that academics have to be insightful enough to know what to take on and discuss and what not to discuss. Professional boundaries must be put in place here to protect and support everyone. Few would disagree that where personal tutoring works, it really works. And both parties clearly benefit from a fulfilling professional development bond between lecturer and student that is based on mutual trust, respect and admiration. However, where it does not work so well, the consequences can be quite distressing for everyone.

Signposting to key services is a must for the personal tutor. Without training and support as a personal tutor, it is daunting and challenging to know when to signpost, but we must see the personal tutor role as being part of the web of relationships that exist between academic departments and professional services teams to support students. Everyone at the university partakes in the student experience and journey. So where academic teams are not working in close collaboration with professional services teams or see themselves and being more committed to other roles and tasks, there are increased risks that students are not supported, and they become acutely aware of this – especially when they realise that some of their peers *are* being supported.

Similar concerns about fairness are sometimes raised across programmes too. In nursing, for instance, few would question the need for students to have this support from a personal tutor who is also a nurse, but 'supporting tutees in clinical practice is fraught with numerous challenges and may even be impracticable' (Watts 2011, 217). However, despite the challenges – which are often based on resource shortages and lack of training around student support – online and/or group tutorials based around well-being and pastoral care may provide a suitable option for many professional disciplines. The needs of students are often simply around having a forum where they feel that they can talk openly about their challenges of being on a particular programme of study. This can be done in groups and online, but where deeper issues are at play and affecting student performance, learning and/or progression, a different approach is needed.

Supporting each other as peers can have other benefits too, such as bringing the group together in a sense of community that is professional, supportive and based on values of care and respect for everyone and their differing experiences. Even though this is not part of a validated curriculum, being together with students in a relatively informal setting where values emerge such as listening, respecting experiences and supporting each other also helps to enhance students' understanding of the need to have values that help and support people generally. Values and good character are key employability skills which are sought after in both the public and private sectors. In this respect, if the case for personal tutoring needed to be made, it could also be said that the experience of being a tutee and having a personal tutor who cares shows how the role can help students to feel at home in the university as well as learn and emulate the values displayed by their personal tutor.

Another positive way of viewing the role of personal tutor is that it opens the minds of academic staff to see students as people and for students to see them as people first and foremost. This can help to break down barriers and insecurities that students may have had about speaking to academic staff. Sometimes we can have a set idea or expectation about a person or a group that may be false. Understanding who academics are and what values they hold as regards students can help students to see that they are respected and cared for at the university and that, although highly qualified and experienced in their field, their lecturers have personal qualities too – such as compassion, empathy and care for students, which may not always be apparent at first glance. Likewise, academics can often live in fear of student feedback and being judged unfairly by students – especially in a climate where students see themselves as customers and often remind staff that they are paying for their education. But getting to know students as people can help to form stronger bonds of trust between these two groups. By seeing things through the lens of the 'other', positive ways forward can be found. Brookfield's work is useful here.

Stephen Brookfield's four lenses is often used in relation to reflective practice in HE roles, but Lochtie et al. have adapted the latter to make it relevant to personal tutoring (p. 162 ff). For Brookfield, every academic tutor must view themselves through four critically reflective lenses, which are the following:

1. Our autobiographies as learners and teachers
2. Our students' eyes
3. Our colleagues' experiences
4. Theoretical literature

(Brookfield 1995, 29–30)

The lenses of student, self, our colleagues, and literature help us to challenge what we might be thinking from merely one perspective (i.e., ourselves) and to re-evaluate or re-think our stances vis-à-vis how to do our role better or how to solve an issue in a more holistic way. Applied to personal tutoring, it can really assist lecturers to see their role as one that requires a holistic overview of multiple perspectives that might be hindering a student's progression and learning and to search for a solution or means of support that includes the four lenses that Brookfield mentions. Keeping a log of personal tutor meetings can help so that we can reflect afterwards (using the 4 lenses) on group tutorials, student focus groups and other meetings to try to determine if various perspectives align or not (Lochtie et al. 2018, 162ff).

This chimes with some of the insights found in a small study of students' experiences of personal tutoring during lockdown. When asked about their experiences of personal tutoring and their expectations, one of the key responses was that they liked tutors to know their story and who they were as people (Mealey 2023, 682ff). There appears to be a reassuring element involved in 'being known' to lecturers on the programme team from the students' perspective. It seems to lead to a greater sense of belonging and confidence. Even if students didn't see their tutor very frequently, especially as they progressed from first year to final year, they felt better knowing that there was an 'open door' of support available to them – even if they didn't access it. Also, we must remember that for the personal tutor, sometimes their biggest resource is themselves and their own story/experiences at university. Students can be greatly inspired to keep going if/when they come to know that even their personal tutor struggled with assignment deadlines or found some aspects of the curriculum difficult or challenging. Our own stories are 'one of the most important sources of insight' (Brookfield 1995, 31).

This of course takes courage and confidence for a new lecturer to speak to students about their own journey into HE and what they found difficult and should not be a requirement in any way. However, showing a human face to students and being open about some of our experiences can be a powerful motivational tool that can inspire students to keep going – especially in times of difficulty. Knowing that others have done something we're trying to do can be hugely inspiring and fill students with hope that they too can achieve what they wish to achieve. And we must give hope as academics!

Decolonising the Curriculum and Personal Tutoring

A further consideration related to support for university students on their learning journey is the need for them to feel that their own personal story and histories are represented in the curriculum. A key concern for students can be that they do not feel that their own identities are valued at university. They feel they may have to leave this identity at the front entrance of the campus building and become someone they are not to feel accepted at university.

These feelings are considered to be part of the kinds of structural inequalities that women and ethnic minorities often speak about when gender pay gaps, inclusive practice in teaching and workplace behaviours are discussed. We know that, for instance, even though we claim that we have become a more inclusive academy that 'ethnic minorities still constitute a minor proportion of senior academic and management staff in most universities' (Begum and Saini 2019, 196). This can suggest to our students that only those from a predominantly white community can realistically progress to senior levels of management in the university structure. In this way, the academic governance itself is symbolic of the inequalities that exist in society and can give the impression to underrepresented groups that their progression in such environments is unlikely. The campaigns to decolonise the curriculum continue based on the obvious gaps that exist in the HE curriculum. For all students to survive in higher education and feel empowered to be all that they can be, they need to feel that their story has value in the approach to teaching taken by academic staff but also in relation to the content that is taught as part of the curriculum.

Following a student demonstration for a decolonised curriculum in South Africa in 2015, for instance, students were calling for artwork to be changed and taken down, the curriculum to be more inclusive and for indigenous knowledge to be considered as a valuable aspect of education. The movement which became known as the #RhodesMustFall movement began in Cape Town and led academics to rethink what the curriculum should be. They key question to be considered was: 'Do [w]e want students to learn predominantly Eurocentric and other Western theories without affording them opportunities to engage with IK [indigenous knowledge] systems?' (Meda 2020, 88–103). It was felt that if students were given the opportunity to engage academically with their own histories and to consider indigenous knowledge as part of their education, it could help to minimise hatred, prejudice and misinformed judgements about race and ethnic minorities.

But 'decolonising the curriculum' is not as straightforward as we might think as there is unlikely to exist a single approach or method of doing this. Scholars have placed the emphasis on different aspects of the curriculum or approaches to reforming it. Some scholars advocate an approach that will help students to treasure history and to replace any content that might promote ideas derived by colonial powers (Le Grange 2016). New ways of knowing that were essentially indigenous ways of knowing are given greater prominence in the curriculum, and diversity is respected more as part of understanding the truth of who we are and what really knowing something entails. Voices that were forgotten or previously not spoken about are now heard and considered. This is extremely powerful for those students and underrepresented groups who may have previously felt that they had to forget their own identities and stories in order to participate and be taken seriously in higher education.

For this reason, too, many are emphasising the importance of including student voices at the design stage of any university curriculum. This is to ensure that students can see themselves in the content and that due consideration is given to any content that might be promoting colonial periods in history and/or frameworks that were exclusionary and prejudicial. Hall et al. (2021) argue that if we are to take race equality in HE seriously, developing effective partnerships with BAME students and staff is a must. In fact, their study showed that it is essential as it challenges neoliberal models of education that are based purely on metrics, numbers and market trends.

Furthermore, involving students in creating a curriculum that is truly geared towards analysing models of history and society that are based on the truth about the past and diverse experiences of events as they played out can help students to develop key critical lenses through which to view societal issues affecting communities of today. It can also help students to be motivated to work for the much-needed changes both in HE and in societies which we may normally wish to avoid as it can involve taking a long and perhaps painful look at the behaviours of the past so that we can grow and learn for the betterment of the future (Hall et al. 2021).

We need to move the academy away from any models of education that might be suggesting that some knowledge, especially that of indigenous or minority groups, is somehow not worthy of consideration on higher education programmes geared towards preparing the elite for the workplace. We also need, as academics, to be constantly challenging our own behaviours, reconsidering what bibliographical materials we give to students to support their learning, and what scholars we choose to focus on in class, for example. This will help not only to ensure that our teaching is inclusive but that it is also placing value on the coexistence of both Western, non-Western and indigenous knowledge together. The constant cycle of questioning and requestioning knowledge from various perspectives is liberating, refreshing and helps to pave the way for a student experience that is more accepting of genuine difference and dialogue with others. When we do this, we enable ourselves and others to look at life through a new lens: one that is more truthful, perhaps more complicated too, and liberating because all voices are heard. Wa Thiong'o (1986) expresses decolonising the curriculum as giving students the opportunity to see themselves clearly in relation to who they are, who others are and the world around them.

In relation to personal tutoring and caring for the well-being of students, all of the mentioned examples are also very relevant. Students need to feel understood. When they approach their tutors for help, support and guidance, it is important that they do not feel less worthy than others asking for help. It is also important if they are asking for guidance on whether to approach an assignment using local knowledge, sources of information or historical perspectives around liberation, oppression or colonialism that they feel celebrated in doing this. If a particular lecture or seminar focuses on a topic from a specifically Western perspective, students may resonate with the topic but from a non-Western perspective. If they are new to higher education, they may feel that their personal understanding of a theme or topic might be less academic because it is derived from their own history, race or religion. This explains further why personal tutors should try to ask students about themselves and how they are getting on with course content. Open conversations with students about their assignments and experiences of certain modules and teaching materials can reveal whether students really understand that localised knowledge and information is also valuable in higher education.

Many universities are redesigning their curricula with equality and diversity and decolonising at the heart of their plans, but the real litmus test as to how effective we are lies with our students. It's now generally accepted and indeed expected that certain key aspects should be present in the design of any new programme such as flexibility to accommodate the busy lives of students, consideration about the inclusive curriculum, designing out any approaches to learning or materials that might promote unconscious bias as well as seeing students as part of every stage of the learning – from the design stage to the assessment.

All of these aspects listed are central to providing a more inclusive education for students, but we need to ensure that once we have designed the curriculum that we are always checking in with our students to find out if they are feeling that these aspects are *genuinely and authentically playing out in their learning*.

Personal tutors can help with his. They can play a role in helping institutions to find out if students are really challenging their own beliefs and prejudices and considering alternative narratives to what they considered or held as truth prior to attending university. Key questions that personal tutors can ask might include: 'Are you feeling that you are receiving an inclusive learning experience?' 'Are you feeling challenged in any way by the curriculum to think differently?' 'Do you think you have changed as a result of studying topics from multiple cultural standpoints, perspectives and backgrounds?' 'Do you feel you're studying a white curriculum?'

Religious Literacy and Personal Tutoring

Linked to the need for personal tutors to ask leading questions about, and offer support for, students regarding the inclusiveness of the curriculum is the need to understand the religious needs of students – particularly in cases where there is a religious observance requirement.

Some students get the impression that faith has no real place in higher education and should not really be spoken about unless they are studying on programmes where questions about religious-based values are relevant or where faith is part of the mission and values strategy of the university. It is often difficult for students (and indeed for some staff) to see how faith and religion might play out in student-related activities, learning and/or support on campus. Additionally, given the stress on the need for inclusiveness, some academics can be quite confused and uncertain about how or whether to discuss religion with students. And of course, with religious literacy decreasing in society more generally many academics and students do not have even a general understanding of world religions.

However, if we are to claim to be supporting the 'whole person' at university – both academically and pastorally – then as academics we need to feel more competent to discuss religious observance and the relationship between the curriculum and religious beliefs with students. This area is largely underdeveloped at present. But we do need to remember that some students are searching for a very different student experience from others. Different student groups have different interests and needs on our campuses – and some of these needs can be spiritual and religious needs.

Understanding what the issues might be is required if we are to claim that personal tutoring offers support to students outside of the purely academic offer. The place of alcohol on campuses, the food choice in eating spaces, the prayer spaces provided for worship can impact on the student experience and be the reason why universities get reputations for being genuinely inclusive or not. But understanding all the complexities surrounding students of faith and their personal as well as environmental needs on campus can be challenging for those who know very little about religion. The Theos Think Tank research on faith and belief on campus stipulates that

> faith and belief societies play hugely important roles on campus in building community, supporting students pastorally and spiritually, and driving social action. However, they often face challenges which limit the contribution they can make to campus life, including their capacity to build bridges across different groups.
> Faith and Belief on Campus: Division and Cohesion –
> Theos Think Tank – Understanding faith. Enriching society

This can mean that some students of faith feel that the 'main' university is not their home as such. They are comfortable within their own group or society, as it has considerable 'bonding social capital.' But they are [frequently] less effective forging wider relationships beyond this group. This can be quite isolating for students who find themselves in this position. But perhaps this is another experience of student life where the role of the personal tutor can be given greater prominence.

We know already that students are more likely to disclose issues to their personal tutor/lecturer as they see this person more than anyone else on the staff team. Furthermore, the bonds of trust can be far greater with the lecturer in the classroom than with other teams or individuals across campus. Given this, personal tutors and academics should try to become familiar with the full range of issues that could potentially impact on how 'at home' a student can feel on campus. Feeling estranged or excluded from the campus or the general environment that is considered to be 'student life' can seem as though it has no place for those students of faith who are searching to continue to live out their faith while being a student in HE. Without an understanding of how to support students of faith, or at least knowing that students might wish to discuss such matters with personal tutors, we cannot really claim to be supporting students in the fullest sense. Nor can we claim to be offering a completely inclusive student experience on campus. This can be worrying when so much resource is being invested in inclusivity and diversity issues more generally. Without efforts to upskill new lecturers and those with developmental needs regarding what we might term as 'religious literacy', students can potentially continue to feel excluded from campus life and report experiences of exclusion and 'micro aggressions' linked to their faith and religious worship needs.

Of course, the obvious training need could be filled with compulsory developmental sessions offered by those skilled in the academic study of world religions, chaplaincy, inter-faith dialogue, ethics and philosophy, for instance. But with many programmes, such as theology and religious studies, struggling to show value for money and sustainability at many universities, the bigger, institutional benefit of having such skilled colleagues on university campuses is often lost from view. We can easily think that we need a very senior appointment to work on equality and diversity more generally and forget the basic need to upskill lecturing staff on these issues as a matter of priority – as it is often in the local contexts, teaching and social spaces that students experience exclusion and feelings of alienation from the dominant student group and subsequently turn to academics for support and help.

Paul Ricoeur: A Model for Personal Tutors Supporting Students of Faith in HE?

In the absence of a suitable model for personal tutoring that can also accommodate the need to discuss and exemplify values around respect for religious observance, we need to look at models that might suggest a way forward. The key issue that seems to lie at the heart of discussions about inclusion of any kind – be that of students with protected characteristics, particular faith-based values or who have come from other parts of the world – is the need to respect 'difference' whilst also being open to the need to provide a shared set of principles ensuring justice and fairness for all students in our universities. This is no easy task, but it is nevertheless vital and necessary – especially in a world where students are keen to see value for money, and their learning experience is now regulated by bodies such as the Office for Students. Indeed, some universities have a designated Office for Institutional Equity, which is tasked with ensuring that all voices on campus are heard and considered and that every decision is fair, transparent and as objective as possible.

A key thinker who has consistently tried to find a middle ground between seemingly conflicting philosophical or moral positions is the French philosopher Paul Ricoeur. Known for trying to adopt a hermeneutical approach to stances taken on issues such as truth and virtue that can cause much tension and division in intellectual communities as well as societies and governments, his work is helpful here. Understanding who we are and who others are in HE is at the heart of the matter concerning how we support students who are different to us – culturally, religiously, ethically or politically. But when we sign up to support students, we are signing up to what can be considered to be a set of values that prompt academics always to seek to respect students without prejudice or the desire to impose one's own beliefs or values on them. Personal tutoring involves exhibiting and living out 'core values' at the university. Lochtie and McIntosh (2018) explain that personal tutors should show students that they uphold and practice values linked to high standards,

84   Who Are Our Students?

'approachability, diplomacy, being non-judgemental, compassion, the "equal partner, not superior" approach, authenticity, [and] valuing students as individuals' (p. 33).

But doing all of this can be difficult if we do not feel able to respect individual differences or respect identities and alterity/otherness. So how do we do this? Following the example of Ricoeur's work on how individual countries could maintain a specific identity while also respecting the need to collaborate and integrate together too is helpful here. Commenting specifically on how Christian communities in particular could do this, he came up with three models to help to find the balance between difference and sameness: (1) the model of translation; (2) the model of exchange of memories; (3) the model of forgiveness.

'The model of translation' refers to the need, where there is potential for misunderstandings to arise, for us to understand other languages firstly but also to have individuals who can help us with integration by providing translations regarding spirituality, faith, cultures and beliefs. We need to understand why people hold certain values or beliefs so that we can support them and enable them to feel part of the culture of a university. We need to be trained as personal tutors to understand what Ricoeur describes as 'the mental universe of the other culture, having taken account of its customs, fundamental beliefs and deepest convictions; in short, the totality of its significant features' (Ricoeur 1992, 108).

Putting ourselves in the position of our students and trying to understand their story, their customs, cultural context and beliefs can help us as tutors to be less judgemental and less ready to blame the students for not understanding and for not engaging properly. Being sensitive to the whole range of academic and, in this case, spiritual and cultural contexts that make up the worldviews of our students is also vital for us to understand in order to support them fully on their intellectual journey.

Ricoeur's second model, 'the model of exchange of memories', refers to the need for integration to include understanding the particular story of a given nation, their rituals, key historical events and their dominant narrative about who they are. He counsels that in relational to transnational integration, we must exercise sympathy toward the 'other culture, even if this is only possible in imaginative terms' (Ricoeur 1996, 6). But when doing this and trying to understand the story of a culture or nation, we also have the responsibility to interpret their story without prejudice or carrying over in our understanding any biases or unhealthy views that may still exist in cultures but which are questionable.

When applied to personal tutoring, we can see how this model can help once again. Understanding the specific story of a student, their country of origin and any relevant events that a student might have witnessed in their life journey can help us to understand that student more deeply. It can be educational for the personal tutor to find out about other cultures from students.

But most importantly, perhaps, it encourages tutors to be mindful of the need *to understand the story* of our students – from multiple perspectives. This can help us to create the conditions and the sense of belonging that students need to feel more at home at university. There may be key founding events that have happened in a student's upbringing that shape how they see the world now, so we should take time to understand where students have come from and what experiences may have marked them significantly on their journey.

Finally, Ricoeur suggests that for harmonious integration, countries also need to adopt a 'model of forgiveness'. Where there have been political tensions, war or colonisation, forgiveness for what might be called the 'wounds of the past' is absolutely necessary in order to create peaceful relations and forge loving bonds between countries and their citizens. When applied to personal tutoring, we must try to remember that in our multicultural societies, tutors from different countries are teaching and giving pastoral support to students from other parts of the world. There is the potential for a tutor to hold a grudge against people from certain countries. Irrespective of what might have happened historically, one's own experiences or one's beliefs, there has to be a sense of forgiveness at play so that we can be fully open and alive to embrace supporting the diverse student body we encounter on our campuses – assuming of course that there is no reason to suspect politically dangerous behaviours or views.

Harbouring resentment for any historical or political reason against students is not helpful – for anyone on campus. Therefore, personal tutors must have training, which includes adopting a stance of forgiveness for any historical wounds they may carry from a previous life experience, and not to react inappropriately if a student's own story triggers any negative or perhaps previously painful experiences.

All of this further highlights the need for training for all personal tutors working in higher education but also the need for these tutors to hold values that are genuinely focussed on the good of students. As Lochtie et al. (2018) put it,

> [values] are central to the decisions [we] make in the lecture theatre, seminar room and while working one-to-one with [our] students. . . . [V]alues are your guiding principles which shape and . . . dictate your . . . behaviours and approach. . . . These should be in line with the 'underlying values of higher education'.
>
> (p. 33)

In other words, everyone should be respected and valued in the HE environment. The well-known theologian and educationalist John Sullivan puts it succinctly when he states that – particularly where institutions are operating from faith-based, values-driven perspectives – when our 'uniqueness and special gifts [are] affirmed and boosted, we are less likely to feel insecure, defensive, or lacking in confidence' (Sullivan 2018, 214–215). Furthermore, citing Theobald's work, Sullivan argues about the importance and value of recognising each individual in our midst at university and in any learning contexts.

He states that the more people generally feel valued and respected as individuals,

> the more they become fitted to enter into collaboration with others . . . and the more that societies and associations make themselves attentive to the resources that each person carries within himself or herself, the more they learn how to tackle flexible the unforeseen eventualities of life.
>
> (Sullivan 2018, 215)

With good personal tutoring and values-driven academic staff on our teams, these benefits are there for the taking by universities who claim to be living out their values through education. This clearly chimes with the literature on personal tutoring that stipulates that while it is quite resource intensive and difficult to quantify in relation to impact and results, it is worthwhile in relation to students feeling valued and cared for as individuals. This sense of 'someone cares for me at the university' has great benefits – including giving students a reason to continue at university and to progress. But this is not really documented in detail by the sector. As Webb et al. (2017) assert, 'despite these studies establishing the importance and value of personal tutoring, few demonstrate the impact in terms of student outcomes' (p. 67).

Personal tutoring is quite costly. But where it is effective, it is highly valued by students. Where the relationship between the personal tutor and the student is less transactional and involves a genuine effort to get to know and support a student, it is a great experience for both parties and often shows the fruits of what treating 'students as partners' could really come to mean eventually – especially where the relationship has been transformative and enhancing for both parties.

In summary, then, the benefits of personal tutoring are many. Where it works well, it has a lasting impact on the lives of the teacher and the student. But in a HE environment which is both complex and demanding in relation to what is expected from a regulatory point of view, sometimes personal tutoring and investment into designing new models to support a new and diverse student demographic is not seen as a top priority. However, as the cost-of-living-crisis begins to be felt by students in higher education, the role of the personal tutor may become more demanding just by virtue of the changes in standards of living and financial arrangements of families that might once have been able to support students in HE. The deeper questions regarding what students should expect to receive at universities given that they are paying for their tuition and experience on campus still remain. What do we consider as value for money in Higher Education? When we talk about the cost of education, do we mean the tuition on its own and the qualification at the end or much more than this?

Or should we place more value on the qualification *and the values and soft skills linked to being a better human being that can be exemplified, passed on and learned through values-driven teaching and personal tutoring in our current HEIs?* How universities will respond to these questions may well depend on the kind of values that both senior leaders at universities hold and the foundational principles upon which our HEIs are built.

Finally, many tutors often say that they do not have time to carry out all of the duties that are currently expected of academics in HE these days. Research, teaching excellence, CPD, personal tutoring, marking, curriculum design and grant applications are all important elements expected of the new and seasoned academic. As one progresses through the career ladder, more administrative positions may be given to staff which takes up more time and energy. This clearly adds to stress levels and can become too much for some. Staying well therefore is very important, as is knowing when to step away from the emails, the requests for help and the guilt surrounding taking a holiday! The final chapter will focus on some key points that will hopefully assist academics in not only surviving but thriving in the current higher education climate.

Bibliography

Advance HE. "Religion and Belief: Researching the Experiences of Staff and Students." 1–123. www.advance-he.ac.uk (accessed 18/12/2022).

Begum, Neema & Rima Saini. 2019. "Decolonising the Curriculum." *Political Studies Review* 17/2: 196–201.

Brookfield, Stephen. 1995. *Becoming a Critically Reflective Teacher.* San Francisco: Jossey-Bass.

Earwaker, J. 1992. *Helping and Supporting Students.* Buckingham: Society for Research into Higher Education and Open University Press.

Guccoine, K. & S. Hutchinson. 2021. *Coaching and Mentoring for Academic Development (Surviving and Thriving in Academia).* Bingley: Emmerald Publishing Ltd.

Hall, Jo, Vedrana Velickovic, & Vy Rajapillai. 2021. "Students as Partners in Decolonising the Curriculum." *Journal of Educational Innovation, Partnership and Change* 7 (1). www.studentengagement.org.uk (accessed 18/12/2022).

Hayman, R. Andy Coyles, Karl Wharton, Erika Borkoles & Remco Polman. 2022. "Undertaking the Personal Tutoring Role with Sports Students at the United Kingdom University." *Journal of Higher Education* 1–14.

Keyes, C.L.M. 2002. "The Mental Health Continuum: From Languishing to Flourishing in Life." *Journal of Health and Social Behaviour* 43: 207–222.

Layman, Rick, Andy Coyles, Karl Wharton, Erika Borkoles & Remco Polman. 2022. "Undertaking the Personal Tutoring Role with Sports Students at a United Kingdom University." *Journal of Further and Higher Education.* https://doi.org/10.10 80/0309877X.2022.2108693 (accessed 08/12/2022).

Le Grange, L. 2016. "Decolonisation Involves More Thank Simply Turning Back the Clock." www.theconversation.com (accessed 18/12/2022).

Lochtie, D., Emily McIntosh, Andrew Stork & Ben Walker. 2018. *Effective Personal Tutoring in Higher Education.* Essex: Critical Publishing.

Mealey, Ann Marie. 2023. "Locked Down but Not Locked Out: Personal Tutoring for Philosophy, Ethics and Religion Students and the Wider Community at Leeds Trinity University During Covid-19." In Md Golam Jamil & Dawn Morley (Eds.) *Agile Learning Environments Amid Disruption: Evaluating Academic Innovations in Higher Education During COVID-19*. Cham, Switzerland: Palgrave Macmillan, 675–690.

Mealey, Ann Marie. 2009. *The Identity of Christian Morality*. Aldershot: Ashgate.

Meda, Lawrence. 2020. "Decolonising the Curriculum: Students' Perspectives." *African Education Review* 17/2: 88–103.

Myers, J. 2008. "Is Personal Tutoring Sustainable? Comparing the Trajectory of the Personal Tutor with That of the Residential Warden." *Teaching in Higher Education* 13/5: 607–611. https://doi.org/10.1080/13562510802334988.

Neuwirth, Lorenz, Svetlana Jovic & Runi Mukherji. 2021. "Reimagining Higher Education During and Post-Covid-19: Challenges and Opportunities." *Journal of Adult and Continuing Education* 27/2: 141–156.

Owen, M. 2002. ' "Sometimes You Feel You're in Niche Time": The Personal Tutor System, a Case Study." *Active Learning in Higher Education* 3/1: 7–23.

Ricoeur, Paul. 1990. *Soi-même comme un autre*. Paris: Edition du Seuil.

Ricoeur, Paul. 1992. "Quel éthos pour l'Europe?" In Peter Koslowski (Ed.), *Imaginer L'Europe: Le marché intérieur européen, tâche culturelle et économique*. Paris: Cerf, 107–116.

Ricoeur, Paul. 1996. "Reflections on a New Ethos for Europe." In Richard Kearney (Ed.) *Paul Ricoeur: The Hermeneutics of Action*. London: Sage Publications, 3–12.

Silver, H. 2004. ' "Residence" and "Accommodation" in Higher Education: Abandoning a Tradition." *Journal of Educational Administration and History* 36/2: 123–133.

Stevenson, Nancy. 2009. "Enhancing the Student Experience by Embedding Personal Tutoring in the Curriculum." *Journal of Hospitality, Leisure, Sport & Tourism Education* 8/2: 117–122.

Sullivan, John. 2018. *The Christian Academic in Higher Education: The Consecration of Learning*. Cham, Switzerland: Palgrave Macmillan.

Theos Think Tank. "Faith and Belief on Campus: Division and Cohesion." *Enriching Society*. https://www.theosthinktank.co.uk/research/2019/07/03/faith-and-belief-on-campus-division-and-cohesion (accessed 11/03/2023).

Tibbetts, Y., J.M. Harackiewicz, S.J. Priniski & E.A. Canning. 2016. "Broadening Participation in the Life Sciences with Social–Psychological Interventions." *CBE— Life Sciences Education* 15/3. https://doi.org/10.1187/cbe.16-01-0001 (accessed 20/05/2023).

Vailes, Fabienne. 2017. *The Flourishing Student: Every Tutor's Guide to Promoting Mental Health, Well-Being and Resilience in Higher Education*. London: Practical Inspiration Publishing.

Walker, Ben. 2018. "A Defining Moment for Personal Tutoring: Reflections on Personal Tutor Definitions and Their Implications." 2–15 (PDF). www.researchgate.net (accessed 20/20/2023). Doi: 10.25507/1120188

Walker, B.W. 2022. "Tackling the Personal Tutoring Conundrum: A Qualitative Study on the Impact of Developmental Support for Tutors. Active Learning in Higher Education." 23/1: 65–77. https://doi.org/10.1177/1469787420926007.

Wa Thiong'o, N. 1986. *Decolonising the Mind: The Politics of Language in African Literature*. Portsmouth: Heinemann.

Watts, T.E. 2011. "Supporting Undergraduate Nursing Students through Structured Personal Tutoring: Some Reflections." *Nurse Education Today* 31/2: 214–218. https://doi.org/10.1016/j.nedt.2010.06.005 (accessed 20/05/2023).

Webb, O., L. Wyness & D. Cotton. 2017. *Enhancing Access, Retention, Attainment and Progression in Higher Education*. https://www.heacademy.ac.uk/system/files/resources/enhancing_access_retention_attainment_and_progression_in_higher_education_1.pdf (accessed 20/05/2023).

Wisker, G., Kate Exley, Maria Antoniou & Pauline Ridley. 2008. *Working One-to-One with Students: Supervising, Coaching, Mentoring, and Personal Tutoring*. New York: Routledge.

Wootton, S. 2006. "Changing Practice in Tutorial Provision within Post-Compulsory Education." In L. Thomas & P. Hixenbaugh (Eds.) *Personal Tutoring in Higher Education*. Stoke on Trent: Trentham Books, 115–125.

Yale, A.T. 2019. "The Personal Tutor-Student Relationship: Student Expectations and Experiences of Personal Tutoring in Higher Education." *Journal of Further and Higher Education* 43/4: 533–544.

Chapter 5

Staying Well in Higher Education

The previous chapter focussed on the need for student well-being in higher education settings and for academic staff to support any personal tutoring approach that may be in place at universities whilst respecting their own professional boundaries too. Khatri and Duggal (2022) put it very well when they assert that multiple interventions on university campuses can help students to feel at home. Leadership and staff development programmes approached from the perspectives of servant and transformational leadership and focussed on developing skills of resilience and well-being; learning analytics and good student-teacher relationships are thought to be key to helping students feel nurtured and cared for in higher education settings (p. 1578).

Citing Tibbetts et al.'s 2016 work, Khatri and Duggal argue that students feel more anxious when they do not feel welcome at their university of choice. They state that: '[t]his is a common emotion for people who come from underrepresented backgrounds. In countries where discrimination and racism are prevalent in educational settings, interventions addressing students' belonging concerns may be necessary, and prudent for research' (Khatri and Duggal 2022, 1579). But what about staff well-being? With all the demands, expectations and moral considerations to take in as a new member of staff on a programme team, it is very easy to forget oneself and to fail to take time to consider what we might need ourselves to stay well and to 'feel at home' at the university. We could feel guilty taking a break from the emails to rest and recuperate during holidays as we might worry that some request to support a student might come while we're on leave, and a 'non-response' might be seen negatively by our superiors.

Although quite uncommon for an introductory book to include reference to the complex area of health and well-being, there continues to be reports from academics that they are paid too little, undervalued and overworked. Work-related stress is often cited as the reason why staff must be signed off work. Often, when this happens, it can be far too late to talk to colleagues about general well-being strategies because the situation has perhaps escalated to the level of seeing a GP or seeking other kinds of professional help.

DOI: 10.4324/9781003168430-6

The intention of this final chapter therefore is to provide some general guidance and share some ideas and themes from the literature on employee well-being in higher education that might help academics to consider their own well-being much more as this is foundational for good job performance as well as overall well-being in life more generally.

Considerations for Well-Being From the Literature: Built Environment

Although it might seem like a strange place to begin to offer some input on staying well in higher education, it is worth mentioning the built environment first. The actual physical environment where academics are working can affect well-being. Besides how we work or how long we are working for, the built environment itself can also affect us – even if we are unaware of this. In a study carried out by Scopelliti et al. (2016), the results showed that people from middle-income groups who interacted with nature to some regular degree showed higher levels of well-being than any other group in the workplace (p. 139).

Those scholars who have studied the urban environment and its impact on stress levels for professionals and those who live in urban areas argue that the built environment can impact on 'individuals' quality of life and well-being' (Scopelliti et al. 2016). Some of the research has demonstrated the adverse impact that urban life/offices or buildings can have on individuals. These environments can be linked – perhaps surprisingly for those who do not work in the field of urban planning – to decreased pro-social actions and motivation as well as negative/aggressive behaviours (Cf. Evans and Stecker 2004).

But the converse is also the case: where there *is* contact with nature, behaviours improve, lower levels of stress are recorded and more positive interactions are recorded (Scopelliti et al. 2016). Even having plants in the office is thought to help. But how many campus leads or estates and facilities teams or senior management teams devote significant time to all of this? It is difficult to say, but it is worthy of consideration as it looks as though some disciplines (which may actually form part of taught provision in universities) have a really detailed grasp of the need for psychical environments to be healthy (to include some aspect of nature within them), geared towards positive work ethics, energetic engagement with the institution, with others and ultimately with oneself. How we feel inside can impact on how we treat students and our colleagues. Without knowing it, if we feel unbalanced and stressed inside, we might unintentionally become the reason why a student feels that they don't belong at university (as we're giving off vibes of not wanting to be disturbed). Sometimes our own feelings of being undervalued or our behaviours due to the impact of stress might be conveying externally a negative message to our managers and colleagues who begin to feel that we are not performing well or contributing positively to the team or to the student experience.

Self-Care and Burnout

This is supported by the literature that has been published on academics and well-being. Velez-Cruz and Holstun (2022) argue that burnout can negatively affect the student experience and lead to a lack of compassion towards students and their needs (p. 119). Where empathy and compassion are lacking, it can be a sign that academics are losing interest or that they are too tired and overworked to see everything that is in front of them and needs attention. The opposite of burnout is known as 'compassion satisfaction'. Compassion satisfaction is thought to exist where professionals get motivated from helping others and really thrive on the feelings of self-worth that come from making a difference at work. Examples include the psychologist who helps their patient to get over a trauma that was holding them back in their life journey or the speech therapist who helps their student to speak with confidence. When we feel as though what we do really matters, it is believed to lead to a satisfaction and sense of achievement that enhances the lives of not only those with whom we interact daily but also our own lives. In short, our well-being improves.

If Covid-19 has taught us anything, it has taught us that health is a priority and that, without it, our entire lives are disrupted. Some scholars refer to the 'great resignation' that happened post-Covid (Sheather and Slattery 2021). Many people reshaped the direction of their careers and their lives by putting health and well-being first. Many of those who previously accepted long commutes to work decided to find other jobs that would enable them to continue working either at home or close to their families so that they could experience a better quality of life.

Although focussed on the American context, the whole concept behind the 'great resignation' is worthy of consideration in all educational contexts. Post pandemic, it is believed that 4.4 million American workers quit their jobs. This indicates clearly that priorities shifted during and after the pandemic and that professionals were viewing both success and their personal priorities and being less about work and more about well-being and quality of life.

Trends in student behaviour post-pandemic seems also to suggest that many students do not really wish to engage with their university campus in the same way as perhaps students did prior to the pandemic. And some of their lecturers are feeling the same way. A large-scale study would need to be carried out to determine the whole range of features that have brought this about and continue to drive certain behaviours in a post-pandemic context, but it is clear that well-being is one of the factors.

What we do know for certain, as Kolomitro et al. (2020) point out, is that academic 'burn-out' is real concern. Many academics see themselves as being continuously on edge 'working hard to gain respect for their contributions, find their place, and keep it' (p. 6). Competing demands, as mentioned in previous chapters, means that often academics are fearful of taking time off or of completely switching off because some task, student concern, query or target might not be met while they are taking rest or winding down. Given this belief and mindset that is common amongst the academics of today, it is often easy to forget the need to take regular breaks, to walk to work, to find time for hobbies, to laugh and enjoy life with friends and/or attend the gym. In fact, the frantic nature of the ever-changing higher education landscape can mean that for conscientious early career academics, there is little time for oneself. And if there is time, this is spent keeping up with research papers, books and conferences because, without these, there is little or no chance of career progression. The phrase 'publish or perish' is heard frequently and often in academic circles, which gives the impression that the failure to publish means that the dream of having a healthy, fulfilling career in academia will be impossible.

So what can we realistically do to help with workplace well-being and to help the academic community to integrate self-care into hectic schedules? Is there any way to achieve career goals and attend to self-care? Are 'compassion satisfaction' and 'workplace well-being' just ideological phrases that are used simply to give the impression that self-care matters to the academic community, or can we make some suggestions as to how they might become more achievable and realistic?

Workplace Well-Being

The literature on workplace well-being suggests multiple ways of looking at the whole concept of workplace well-being. Some of the models fit nicely with the concepts of *eudaimonic* well-being, while others tend to be more focussed around satisfaction of basic needs that an individual might have.

Some of the literature links workplace well-being with the concept of 'happiness' itself, but it is difficult to see how helpful this can be to the new academic when the idea of happiness is so unique to the individual. It would be quite difficult to arrive at a shared understanding. Also, what we might find happiness in today can change over time, so no matter how one views workplace well-being, the concept of what makes us happy is ever changing, thereby making it difficult to make the concept in any way the benchmark for measuring workplace well-being. As Cynthia D Fisher points out, '[e]udaimonic approaches are linked to the satisfaction of basic human needs for competence, autonomy, relatedness, and self-acceptance' (p. 11).

Fisher's quote indicates that, in spite of limitations, there is something very worthy of consideration here though in these kinds of approaches as often, when we are starting a new role or job, we worry about how people are viewing us from the outside. Common questions include: How will I fit in? Who will decide on how I am performing? Will they like me? Should I step up and suggest 'other' approaches or just leave things as they are and try to make others happy around me so that I'm accepted into the team? Often our focus is on how others might be seeing us, to the detriment of how we are also treating and seeing ourselves. The positive aspects of eudaimonic approaches may well be therefore that they encourage us to focus on our own growth, purpose and meaning in life so that

94   Staying Well in Higher Education

we can continue to find ways of working and living based on the concepts of self-empowerment, self-actualisation and virtue (Cf. Sheldon and Elliot 1999).

One of the reasons why academics often get disaffected in the workplace is due to the fact that they can sometimes begin to feel that their authentic purpose is somehow being undermined at work. When we are realising what we truly believe is our purpose in life, we feel better. We feel positive, upbeat, enthusiastic and happy to be part of the team that we are in, which seems to share in the purpose to serve students and to be excellent in all that we do as academics. Frequently, we hear academics expressing dissatisfaction when their role changes or some strategic level decision is made which they believe will affect them and/or their students adversely. The dissatisfaction arises really from the fact that they feel that a particular initiative can affect their purpose and how they see that can best be done for their students.

This chimes well with Ryff et al.'s work in which well-being is thought to have six dimensions – all of which are linked to how we feel at work and our overall sense of well-being in that context. The dimensions are self-acceptance, purpose in life, environmental mastery, positive relationships, personal growth and autonomy (Cf. Ryff 1989, 1069ff).

Broadly speaking, if we reflect on these areas of life, we can see that it makes sense to see how the absence of one of these elements can lead to such dissatisfaction in the workplace and in life in general. More specifically, if what we believe our essential 'purpose' in the workplace is something other than how our manager or colleagues see it, we can feel alienated, 'othered', isolated and alone on the team.

The Need for Transformational Leadership in HE

This explains why the concept of 'transformational leadership' matters so much in professional life across all sectors but particularly in the highly structured and regulated HE environment. We can often feel as though we are constantly trying to meet the latest sector demand for accountability for standards or excellence and quickly forget what is happening to our academics as they are trying to respond in an agile way to new developments.

In this model of leadership, there is a stress placed upon the behaviours that leaders should exhibit to foster the well-being of their staff, ensure that motivation is at its highest and that all members of the team are given what might be termed 'individualized consideration' (Bass and Riggio 2006, 242). This is the reason why this particular approach to leadership is considered to be so important: as it allows and expects managers to know their staff and to focus on what an individual might need to allow them to function and to develop positively in their working environment. Far too often, especially when one is on a fixed-term academic contract or just covering a module for a professor who is on research leave, we can feel that nobody knows us on the staff team – least of all our line manager, who seems to be overloaded with work and constantly in meetings with permanent members of staff. The status of a new academic can sometimes mean that they are not in the team meetings, and so it can be difficult for them to get to know how things work or feel appreciated or known as a person because they are not really (or at least not yet) part of the full-time, permanent team.

But if the model of transformational leadership teaches us anything, it teaches us that every member of staff who contributes should be encouraged to think of themselves as a key part of the healthy operational functioning of the team. 'Transformational leadership is inherently positive because of its focus on ethical behaviour (idealized influence), elevating employees' motivation (inspirational motivation), encouraging and allowing employees to think for themselves (intellectual stimulation) and demonstrating real concern for individuals' needs (individualized consideration)' (Bass and Riggio 2006, 242).

This kind of model sits in stark contrast to models of leadership or individual approaches to academic leadership that seem to be more 'laissez-faire' or based on a notion that 'if they are doing their Ph.D and know the subject then they don't really need much more help to get on with the teaching that they have been given'. But experience of talking to new staff and leading Advance HE accredited PGCERTHE provision shows that there is quite a significant transition to be made for staff from the point when they are hired for a new job to the point where they feel accepted, comfortable and confident to 'find their way' and progress in the world of HE. In fact, the move from full-time research into teaching undergraduate students for the first time can be even more challenging as the transition from research to teaching can be great.

The surprise that comes when a new colleague realises that students need a lot of support, or that the standard is not what the academic expected at third level, or that there are so many quality assurance, or TEF-related, protocols and expectations to follow and deliver on any validated curriculum can be quite big. This alone shows that everyone needs support and help. Mentoring can be a great way to make positive and confident steps forward but 'feeling supported' more generally by the manager and team members is perhaps the most important aspect that can help us to feel better.

Where we are constantly worried and/or guessing or hoping that how we are doing things will turn out to be correct, stress increases and workplace well-being is consequently often affected. The worry and anxiety that staff can feel may impact on how they see themselves as a person and as an academic. And having the courage to ask for help and support might cause the additional stress and worry about being judged by academic peers who seem to have it all under control!

Managing our 'Stress Bucket'

But how therefore can we begin to take control? The NHS, for instance, promotes an activity that is often useful for managers and academics to do on a regular basis. This is called 'The Stress Bucket' (OHC_StressBucket.pdf (hey. nhs.uk)). It is derived from the idea that each of us experiences stress at certain times in our lives and that this is quite normal. Events in our lives often lead us to feeling worn-out and lacking in motivation and drive. Home-life, family issues, our finances and work itself can often be the reasons why we feel overloaded and 'burned out'. What stresses people out will vary from person to person, but it is very important for us to know and to understand when our 'stress-bucket' is becoming too full and is about to overflow. It is therefore our own personal responsibility to know when a situation is becoming too much for us to handle and manage.

When our 'stress-bucket' is starting to get too full, we might begin to feel lacking in motivation and drive, snappy, irritable, fatigued, low and/or tearful. These could be signs that we need to take some time out to reconsider what we are doing in our lives, how we are doing it, and try to move towards a different set of circumstances which will be less stressful and more supportive vis-à-vis our own well-being and health.

The metaphor of the bucket helps us to think about when a bucket might be full with water and could overflow. When our stress is high, our stress-bucket could be overflowing and we could end up being ill. There can be a need to adopt some 'positive coping strategies' at this point, in order to get the water in our 'stress-buckets' back to a more manageable level. Put differently, we need to see where the taps are in our lives so that, when needed, we can open them and allow the stress to pour out.

But techniques that work seem to be quite individual and depend upon what each of us enjoys doing to relax and recuperate after stressful situations arise in our lives. 'Emptying our stress-bucket' is something that we must do in order to live a more fulfilling life. Activities such as socialising, meditating, reading, taking nice baths, walking in the countryside and even having the courage and inner strength to ask for help are all part and parcel of what we need to do regularly to stay healthy and well ourselves. After all, if we neglect this, how can we continue to support students? How can we continue to break the barriers to new knowledge and understanding? How can we go forward confidently in our professional careers if we are constantly feeling drained or not fully present to ourselves and to others? The first step therefore is to look after ourselves before we can look after others.

From experience, however, many academics would say that they just 'don't have a life.' In fact, many professionals tend to glorify overworking and somehow make it the badge of honour that successful people should have. However, if we think of how many of our professional colleagues we have seen having to take significant amounts of time off to recover from being burned out and stressed out, we will know how devastating this can be for that person.

It can be difficult to really let go of work and rest and to encourage the person who is ill and needing to rest to stop worrying about what is going on at work while they are on sick leave. The feelings are quite difficult to manage alongside the actual physical and mental challenges that come with being stressed to the point of burnout.

Being proud of 'not having a life' is something we may need to reconsider. We need to continuously ask ourselves if our lives are fulfilling? Are we trying to combine good health with our professional success? Or are we simply attending to health in a reactive sense only when we get ill and are not taking the steps to live well on a daily basis?

At this point, it is important to say that all of us will experience well-being differently. We enjoy different things. Our hobbies and interests are unique to us as people, so how we spend our leisure time will be up to us alone. The key thing is that we do in fact make time for hobbies and interests, sports or enjoyable trips to the countryside and local parks. The more fulfilled we feel, the more likely we will feel able to face the daily challenges that arise that could otherwise throw us off course.

But this is not to say that staying well in HE is always *only* up to us. There are also institutional considerations that universities should think about too. In their article on 'Burnout and Work Engagement of Academics in Higher Education Institutions', Barkhuizen et al. (2014) argue that universities have at least two clear interventions that they can adopt to help with workplace well-being. They argue that '[. . .] higher education should implement interventions to decrease burnout and increase work engagement' and make 'role clarity' and the need to include 'variety' and 'learning opportunities' into the academic's day-to-day routine (p. 331).

Smarter working patterns and meetings with very clear, focussed agendas, outcomes and actions can help everyone to feel in the loop regarding key decisions and/or expectations. Efficiently run meetings can also help as they can help to avoid the need for more meetings where long discussions which are off-topic take place with few outcomes or tangible results. We need to get better at *leading for well-being* too. Attending meetings prepared and ready to contribute effectively can help to keep spirits high and focussed on the right things. Maintaining effective relationships between leaders and staff is also key here. Good leadership and values-driven approaches to leading staff often help academics to feel valued for their contributions and respected – irrespective of rank. Far too often we can be worried as a new academic that our contribution will be seen negatively or that it might sound silly or that we will somehow be considered as an imposter. Again here, studies on transformational leadership styles suggest that there is a link between how we lead staff teams and how they feel about themselves and their job (Samad et al. 2020). Indeed, some researchers argue further that where organisations invest in specific employee well-being programmes and promote literacy around staying well, greater business benefits have also been reported (McCarthy et al. 2011). Although

98 Staying Well in Higher Education

well-being should be seen as being of value in and of itself, it is positive that a further benefit can be seen from this research: where people are well, performance is also better.

Spirituality and Well-Being

Aside from the importance for academics – and all professionals for that matter – to find self-care activities outside of work that can help minds and bodies to rest and recuperate and find fulfilment in all areas of life, there are also benefits (for those who search for these) in turning to one's spirituality for help. Many professionals profess a faith, and some – while not practicing a faith – admit to having a spiritual life.

But for all the interest there is shown in spirituality and spiritual practices today, there continues to be debate, discussion and uncertainty about how exactly we define spirituality. Generally speaking, though, we can say that when people search for and acknowledge a faith, they are admitting that there are dimensions of reality available to us that we do not see and that, for those who seek these, engaging in healthy spiritual activities can help individuals because they are oriented towards 'wholeness' of a person and authentic living (McGinn et al. 1985, 14–15).

The issue with spirituality, for some, is that it is so broad that it can take on negative connotations and lead to negative interpretations if it is not always brought into dialogue with the lens of ethics, morality and virtue. The concern here is based on the fact that many spiritual practices involve a focus only on the self, and there may be reason to believe that they foster individualism. The well-known theologian Sandra Schneiders argues that the mere range of spiritual traditions and practices that exist makes it even more difficult to even agree on a definition, let alone to say or to distinguish which forms of spirituality are healthy and which are not (Schneiders 1986, 224–225). But still, the concepts of wholeness, moving towards the fullness of being, and the idea of embracing a fuller life seem to be common themes in most accepted definitions of spirituality. We can clearly see therefore how the concepts of authenticity and self-care and holistic activities could link to well-being for those who seek it through the lens of their spiritual life. Spirituality is thought to involve a sincere attempt to become more whole and sincere about the direction and goals of our life, and we pursue these purposefully and peacefully. And we can use it in that respect to guide our life and to nurture how we stay well and cope with the pressures of life and of work. Feeling good and loved on the inside can help us to emanate positivity and kindness on the outside too. And people often respond very well to all of this.

For some, fostering a sense of well-being and authentic living also involves religious worship, prayer and faith. Spirituality has become very attractive for many people as a way of staying grounded in who they are outside of the pressures of work. Spiritual people tend to find ways of living that help them

Staying Well in Higher Education 99

to make sense of their feelings and experiences, to find peace where they feel they were initially seeking to find vengeful ways of 'getting back at someone' at work and to put their own place in the world into a sacred space where they acknowledge gratitude for the things that they do have and hope for the things to come that will be positive in their lives.

Some individuals keep a prayer journal or a spirituality diary to make notes of their journey, their week, their feelings, who they need to forgive and how they need to start the following week wearing a lens of love on their eyes while seeking excellence and authenticity in all that they do on a daily basis.

Learning how to manage our feelings can be a key to managing difficult relationships at work, especially with those individuals who always wish to be right and seem unwilling to see others (as people) or their opinions as being of importance other than as a means of reaching a KPI or a target. As stated previously, transformational leadership links with this perspective as it encourages all – whether spiritual or not – to really 'see' people on a team as individuals and to respect them as people in order to get the most out of them and develop their potential more fully. In 2009, and on a secondment with CAFOD, the well-known theologian Celia Deane-Drummond pointed out that there is a disconnectedness in a lot of models of living in today's world, even in models of so-called development, which should have human beings at their centre. Concerned specifically about how we are living in relation to the environmental crisis, she calls for a reflection on what we are using in our lives to 'fill the void' (Deane-Drummond 2009, 57). This is a question, however, that needs to be asked in relation to workplace well-being and academic life more generally too. We need to ask ourselves, 'How am I filling the void?' 'What really matters to me?' 'Am I living the best life I could be?' 'Or am I blaming my feelings of stress on factors that I can genuinely change?' 'Do I need to make some small changes every day for my own well-being which I will eventually see rippling out to my students and bringing about positive change in their lives as well as in my own?'

The key factor to remember here is that our well-being in higher education does impact on those we serve as well as on ourselves. Therefore, it matters a great deal, and we need to make it a priority or at the very least begin to help individuals to reflect on finding ways of supporting their own well-being, which will enable them to live well at the university for themselves and for the students. So it is all a worthwhile venture really when we break it down to reminding ourselves that we are always in a web of relationships with others. The more we can work on being the best version of ourselves in work and at home, the more fulfilling our lives will be for us and for those around us – including for our students.

Finally, it is important to remember that whatever way we approach our academic life, we need to find peace within ourselves, a set of values that will guide our interactions with others and other academics in the community who can support and guide us. After all, we are meant to be engaged in a community of practice. And communities are meant to be supportive, kind and nurturing spaces where we can grow safely and confidently. Fearne Cotton's book *Calm* encourages us all to find 'magic places' (Cotton 2017, 189). These places, for her, are the places where we feel peaceful and serene, grounded and safe. We owe it to ourselves in our busy HE environments to find our 'magic place', our library of words and phrases and books and/or activities that still bring that spark to our lives and our imaginations and remind us of the 'why?' of higher education in the first place. We sometimes need, for our own well-being, to come back to the 'magic place' where we decided we wanted to make a difference to the lives of students and people who might wish to transform their lives through university education. Keeping our purpose in mind can be a great reminder to keep going, that teaching is still a noble vocation and that, as much as we complain about them, we love teaching our students! I teach therefore I am!

Bibliography

Barkhuizen, Nicolene, Sebastian Rothmann & Fons J.R. van de Vijer. 2014. "Burnout and Work Engagement of Academics in Higher Education Institutions: Effects of Dispositional Optimism." *Stress Health* 30: 322–332.

Bass, B.M. & R.E. Riggio. 2006. *Transformational Leadership*. Hillsdale, NJ: Erlbaum, 2nd edn.

Cotton, Fearne. 2017. *Calm*. London: Orion Publishing Group.

Deane-Drummond, C. 2009. *Seeds of Hope: Facing the Challenge of Climate Justice*. London: CAFOD Publications.

Evans, G.W. & R. Stecker. 2004. "Motivational Consequences of Environmental Stress." *Journal of Environmental Psychology* 24/2: 143–165.

Fisher, Cynthia D. 2014. "Conceptualizing and Measuring Well-Being at Work." In Peter Y. Chen and Cary L. Cooper (Eds.), *Well-being: A Complete Reference Guide*. Oxford: Wiley Blackwell, Vol. III, 9–34.

Khatri, P. & H.K. Duggal. 2022. "Well-Being of Higher Education Consumers: A Review and Research Agenda." *International Studies of Consumer Studies* 1564–1593.

Kolomitro, Klodifana, Natasha Kenny & Suzanne Le-May Sheffield. 2020. "A Call to Action: Exploring and Responding to Educational Developers Workplace Burnout and Well-Being in Higher Education." *International Journal for Academic Development* 25/1: 5–18. tandfonline.com (accessed 26/12/2022).

McCarthy, G., S. Almeida & J. Ahrens. 2011. "Understanding Employee Well-Being Practices in Australian Organizations." *The International Journal of Health, Wellness and Society* 1/1: 181–197.

McGinn, Bernard, John Meyendorff & Jean Leclerq (Eds.). 1985. *Christian Spirituality: Origins to the Twelfth Century*. New York: Crossroads.

OHC_StressBucket.pdf. www.hey.nhs.uk.

Ryff, C. 1989. "Happiness Is Everything, or Is It? Explorations on the Meaning of Psychological Well-Being." *Journal of Personality and Social Psychology* 57: 1069–1081.

Samad, A., M. Murchiri & S. Shahid. 2020. "Investigating Leadership and Employee Well-Being in Higher Education." *Leadership and Employee Well-Being* 57–76.

Schneiders, Sandra. 1986. "Theology and Spirituality: Strangers, Rivals, or Partners?" *Horizons* 13/2: 224–225.

Scopelliti, M., G. Carrus, C. Adinolfi, G. Suarez, G. Colangelo, R. Lafortezza, A. Panno & G. Sanesi. 2016. "Staying in Touch with Nature and Well-Being in Different Income Groups: The Experience of Urban Parks in Bogotá." *Landscape and Urban Planning* 148: 139–148.

Sheather, J. & D. Slattery. 2021. "The Great Resignation: How Do We Support and Retain Staff Already Stretched to Their Limit." *British Medical Journal* 375: 2533–2534. https://doi.org/10.1136/bmj.n2533 (accessed 26/12/2022).

Sheldon, K.M. & A.J. Elliot. 1999. "Goal Striving, Need Satisfaction, Longitudinal Well-Being: The Self-Concordance Model." *Journal of Personality and Social Psychology* 76: 482–497.

Velez-Cruz, Ramon J. & Vasti P. Holstun. 2022. "Pandemic Impact on Higher Education Faculty Self-Care, Burnout, and Compassion Satisfaction." *The Journal of Humanistic Counseling* 61: 118–127.

Conclusion

As the HE sector continues to grow and change, all academics will need to see themselves as part of a continuous cycle of growth and change. Adapting to change might be more difficult depending on what it is that we are expected to do or to change about our teaching practice.

The task is never-ending. And therefore our commitment to providing excellence in all areas of our work at the university is crucial. Whenever we feel ourselves diving into a cycle of negativity or complacency, we need to ask ourselves again and again: 'What is my purpose in HE?' 'Who am I for students at the university?' 'Why do I do what I do?' and 'Why does it matter that I do it well?'

When we re-engage with our primary purpose at times, it can help us to become more positive and resilient when we are faced with challenges or expected to complete tasks which we personally do not see value in. This is where our personal and professional values come into play in each instance. If we are teaching in higher education, we have to always remember that we are providing a service to our students and a commitment to see their progression through to graduation and beyond if they wish to continue to further studies. People's futures are in our hands to a certain extent.

How we treat students as individuals really matters therefore, not least because they are fee-paying but because their future depends in part on our professionalism, teaching and support. Our enthusiasm and passion for our subject, our overall approach, our clarity of expression as regards assessment and demystifying the rules of the game, and our values are on display for students every time we interact with them. This is both a privilege and a responsibility that we need to take on while always keeping in mind that the success of our students is our own success and vice versa. We work hand in hand trying to make sense of learning, of difficult knowledge, of assessment, of student issues and needs and of our own roles within that. At times it might seem complex, even messy and scary. But it is often within the confusion and complexities that we see the seeds of hope.

When it boils down to it, our universities and the staff in them just want to do good. And in order to do good, we must always find ways of doing more

DOI: 10.4324/9781003168430-7

good for our students and of pursuing our vocation to teach as part and parcel of the pursuit of good in the world. Integrated classrooms where respect and values of inclusiveness and compassion are supporting diverse student communities learning together in peace and understanding are a beacon of hope to a fractured and divided world. They give us a prophetic glimpse of how society could be if we reflected carefully together on how to combine 'identity' and 'alterity' together – as academics have to do in each and every class that they teach. We also have a duty to do good for ourselves by taking time out when needed and finding ways of living a fulfilling and happy professional and personal life.

It's a tricky balancing act. But when our core values align with our work, that's when we feel most fulfilled and ready to make things happen because we see why they matter. When we show justice, fairness, transparency, integrity and a commitment to making each and every student feel supported and welcome in the HE environment (no matter who they are or where they come from), meeting a teaching excellence KPI does not seem like a burden. Rather it feels more like a natural extension of doing what is right for successful education for all.

In order to know, however, how to act consistently for good as an academic, we need to always be involved in the community of practice that is trying to find sector-leading ways of teaching an ever-changing student demographic, but, most importantly, we need to be open to the student voice that is always inviting us to re-think, re-plan, re-focus, and re-examine what we previously thought to be the 'way to do things'.

It is this student voice, which we sometimes hear loudly in our NSS data, or as a quiet whisper for help when a student has the courage to tell their personal tutor what they need to succeed on their programme, that is our compass towards finding the truth about what successful teaching looks like in every age.

And remember with each passing year that we meet a new group of uncertain students on the first day at university that they are trusting in us and in our ability to help them to realise their dreams. Having empathy is key to them settling in and believing that they belong in HE. Therefore, '*tread gently*'.

Epigraph

I dedicate this book to the Mealey Family, the Sisters of the Cross and Passion order, and the entire Leeds Trinity University Community (management, academic and professional services staff, students, alumni and distinguished friends of the university) who have walked the journey with me professionally and personally since I was first appointed as a lecturer in 2005.

Thank you for all that you have taught me about myself, about learning and teaching and the need to always try to develop the inherent potential of everyone.

With love and gratitude, always.

Ann Marie.

LTU – 'Training Teachers Since 1966'

Index

Archer-Kuhn, B. 58
Ariew, R. 7
Aristotle 6, 18
assessment and feedback 10, 62–63;
    Assessment Compact 61–62;
    being authentic and 45–49; fair
    and value-driven 49–52; 'Impacts
    of Higher Education Assessment
    and Feedback Policy and
    Practice on Students: A Review
    of the Literature 2016–2021'
    on 43, 44–45; introduction to
    43; religion, belief and 52–55;
    tailored approach to, with Jisc
    55–56
assignment unpacking 50–51
Aune, K. 54
authentic assessment 45–49
autonomy 75

BAME students 66, 79
Barkhuizen, N. 97
Bell, L. 15
blog posts 10
Bols, A. 60
Brookfield, S. 77
built environment 91
burnout 92–93

Calm 100
Carless, D. 60
Cartesian philosophy 6–7
class debates 10
coaching 70–71
cognitive challenge in authentic
    assessment 48–49
common good 6
conscious incompetence 57, 61

constructivism 10
Cotton, F. 100
Covid-19 19, 92
critical thinking 48
Crook, C. 51
curriculum: decolonised 78–81; design
    of 12–13

David, V. 52
Deane-Drummond, C. 99
decolonised curriculum 78–81
Descartes, R. 6–7
digital learning 9, 10, 13, 19
Duggal, H. K. 90
Dweck, C. 8

Earwaker, J. 69
'Effective Assessment in a Digital Age'
    55–56
enthusiasm 19
entrenchment of privilege 14
environmental mastery 75
ethics 15–16
eudaimonic well-being 93

fairness 49–52; personal tutoring
    and 76
Fazey, D. 18
feedback *see* assessment and feedback
feed-forward 59–60, 62
Field, J. 15
Fisher, C. D. 93
500 Tips on Assessment 56
Ford, H. 19

goal-orientation 18
great resignation 92
groupwork 9

happiness 74
Hayman, R. 72
HEA Feedback Toolkit 58
HEFCE (Higher Education Funding Council for England) 14
higher education: authentic assessment in 45–49; challenges of demands in 3–4, 102–103; ethics in 15–16; how students learn and purposes of 6–11; model for personal tutors supporting students of faith in 83–87; from perspective new lecturer 4–5; staff well-being in (*see* well-being, staff); transformational leadership in 94–95
Holland, S. 58
Holstun, V. P. 92

Jisc 55–56

Kahoot 9, 13
Kessler, G. 19
Keyes, C. L. M. 74–75
Khatri, P. 90
knowing versus learning 8–9
knowledge, tacit 14–15
'Knowledge Its Own End' 6
Kolomitro, K. 92

Land, R. 11
Lea, M. R. 59
leadership, transformational 94–95
leading questions 9
learning: assessment of 9–11; curriculum design for 12–13; digital 9, 10, 13, 19; enthusiasm for 19; good practice in 8; knowing versus 8–9; modular 11–12, 18; purpose of 6–7; scaffolded 61; in search for truth 6–7; situated 56; social mobility, skills gap and 7, 18–19; student motivation for 16–19; students as partners in 13–14; student surveys on 7–8; tacit knowledge 14–15; taking time 11–16; *see also* personal tutoring
lecturers: advice for new 13; as catalysts for learning 17; fair and values-driven 49–52; looking at things from perspective of new 4–5;

trust in 58–59; well-being of (*see* well-being, staff)
life experiences 10
life satisfaction 75
Lochtie, D. 83–84, 85

MacKinnon, S. 58
McDowell, S. 59
McIntosh, E. 83–84
Mentimeter 9
Mentkowsky, M. 51
Meyer, J. H. F. 11
model of translation 84
Montgomery, L. 59
Moodle 10
motivation, student 16–19
MS Forms 10
MS Teams 10, 60
Myers, J. 73

National Student Survey (NSS) 7–8
National Union of Students (NUS) 60
Neary, M. 13
Neuwirth, L. 73
Newman, J. H. 6, 7, 18

O'Neill, G. 46–47
online quizzes 10

personal growth 75
personal tutoring 66–68; barriers to progress in 72–78; challenges to adopting a university-wide system for 71–72; coaching model of 70–71; decolonising the curriculum and 78–81; as individualised learning 69; models of 69–71; Paul Ricoeur and potential model for supporting students of faith in higher education and 83–87; professional model of 70; religious literacy and 81–83; *see also* learning
Pitt, E. 44, 47
Polanyi, M. 14
positive affect 74
positive functioning 75
positive relations with others 75
Postgraduate Certificate in Teaching and Learning in Higher Education (PGCERTHE) 5

Post-it Note exercises 9, 13
pre-professional identity 57–58
Price, M. 61
Principles of Philosophy 6–7
professional model of personal tutoring 70
purpose in life 75

Quality Assurance Agency for Higher Education 55–56; Subject Benchmarks for Theology and Religious Studies 54, 58
question and answer sessions 10
Quinlan, K. 44, 47

Race, P. 10, 11, 56; on motivation and keeping students going 16–19
realism 47
Reconceptualising Feedback in Higher Education 51
religious beliefs: model for personal tutors supporting students' 83–87; personal tutoring and 81–83; religious literacy and 52–55, 66–67; well-being and 98–100
Ricoeur, P. 66, 67; model for personal tutors supporting students of faith in higher education 83–87
Rust, C. 62
Ryff, C. 94

scaffolded learning 61
Schneiders, S. 98
Scopelliti, M. 91
self-acceptance 75
self-care 92–93
simulations 47
situative learning 56
skills gap 7, 18–19
social acceptance 75
social actualization 75
social capital 49, 82
social coherence 75
social constructivism 56
social contribution 75
social integration 75
social mobility 7

spirituality and well-being 98–100
Stevenson, H. 13, 73
Street, B. V. 59
stress-bucket 96–98
students: assessment of (*see* assessment and feedback); BAME 66, 79; enthusiasm in 19; motivation in 16–19; as partners 13–14; personal tutoring of (*see* personal tutoring); religious beliefs of 52–55, 66–67; trust from 58–59; valued for who they are 52–55
Sullivan, J. 85–86
Sykes, E. 52

tacit knowledge 14–15
Theos Think Tank 82
Tibbetts, Y. 90
transformational leadership 94–95
transparency in authentic assessment 49
trust 58–59
truth, search for 6–7
Turnitin 43, 45
tutoring *see* personal tutoring

unconscious incompetence 57, 61

Vailes, F. 57, 61, 72
values-driven academics 49–52
Velez-Cruz, R. J. 92
Vevoz quizzes 9, 13
virtues, promotion of 6

Walker, B. 69–70
Wa Thiong'o, N. 80
Watts, T. E. 71
Webb, O. 86
well-being, staff 90–91; literature on built environment and 91; managing the 'stress bucket' and 96–98; need for transformational leadership in higher education and 94–95; self-care and burnout and 92–93; spirituality and 98–100; in the workplace 93–94
Wicklow, K. 60
Wisker, G. 70, 75

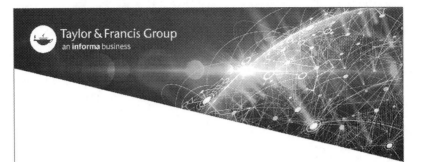

Printed in the United States
by Baker & Taylor Publisher Services